G U N P O W D E R

ABOUT THE AUTHOR

Harneet Baweja and his wife Devina Seth grew up in Kolkata, and from an early age food played an important role in both their families as they enjoyed recipes that had been passed down for generations. They moved to London in 2014 and set up Gunpowder restaurant with head chef Nirmal Save. Nirmal is originally from Mumbai, where he grew up on a farm and developed a keen interest in the ingredients and produce his mother and grandmother taught him to cook.

www.gunpowderlondon.com   Instagram: @gunpowder_london   Twitter: @gunpowder_ldn

GUNPOWDER

EXPLOSIVE FLAVOURS
FROM MODERN INDIA

HARNEET BAWEJA,
DEVINA SETH AND NIRMAL SAVE

Photography by Peter Cassidy

KYLE BOOKS

TO MOTHERS AND GRANDMOTHERS

An Hachette UK Company
www.hachette.co.uk

First published in Great Britain in 2018 by
Kyle Books, an imprint of Kyle Cathie Ltd
Carmelite House
50 Victoria Embankment
London EC4Y 0DZ
www.kylebooks.co.uk

ISBN 978 0 85783 438 6

The publishers would like to thank
Rachel de Thample for her contribution

Project Editor: Tara O'Sullivan
Copy Editor: Vicki Murrell
Editorial Assistant: Sarah Kyle
Designer: Evi O. / Evi O. Studio
Typesetting: Jo Wright and Susan Le / Evi O. Studio
Photographer: Peter Cassidy*
Illustrator: Our Place
Food Stylist: Aya Nishimura
Prop Stylist: Iris Bromet
Production: Nic Jones and Gemma John
*see page 192 for additional photo credits

A Cataloguing in Publication record for this title is
available from the British Library.

Printed in China

10 9 8 7 6 5 4 3 2 1

INTRODUCTION

Indian food is a vast treasure trove. It is a unique collection of multiple cultures and centuries-old recipes handed down and personalised by every household. My wife Devina, Head Chef Nirmal Save and I have carefully collected the gems and jewels of our families' kitchen secrets to create Gunpowder, a home-style Indian kitchen restaurant. Now, we have gathered them into this book to share with you.

OUR INDIAN STORY

Growing up in Kolkata, I was surrounded by the mingling flavours and aromas of my family's cooking and the city's street food. School days were rounded off with queuing for *pani puri*, an enormously popular snack of hollow *puri*, fried until crisp and filled with tamarind chutney, chaat masala, potato or chickpeas – delicious sweet, spicy and sour flavours that we enjoyed together, standing or sitting with family and friends. Then we would rush home to Maa's Kashmiri Lamb Chops. These beautifully spiced chops remain one of my favourite foods, and you can find the recipe on page 104.

Devina is also from Kolkata and our lives very much interlinked around the Indian foods of the city. Her mother and grandmother cooked delectable meals that they created and adapted in their own ways. Devina undertook an education and career away from the kitchen, but even with a degree in journalism and a Masters from Goldsmiths, University of London, the craving for the cuisine of Kolkata never faded for her, such as fond memories of her best-loved comfort food *kichdi* – a mix of rice and lentils that her granny made for her growing up.

Kolkata is a cultural and intellectual hub, buzzing with Ambassador taxis whizzing past, swarms of people going about their daily lives and the hum of ever-popular street food vendors offering piping hot delicacies. The city has an abundance of market stands and food stalls such as Dacres Lane, where my wife and I have whiled away hours trying every creation you can think of, from traditional Bengali *ghugni* (dried white peas mixed with tamarind, chillies and jaggery) to Bengali's own take on Chinese chow mein, which uses turmeric and chicken masala for a twist on the original.

Originally from Mumbai, Nirmal was born into a family of second-generation farmers. He began cooking alongside his mother and grandmother at just 12 years old. They introduced him to a variety of regional dishes and flavours, and passed on their closely guarded recipes. Growing up on the farm ensured that he was surrounded by fresh produce, spending his hours catching game, digging up vegetables and collecting fruit from the Sapodilla trees, thus instilling in him a lifelong appreciation of cooking with fresh ingredients.

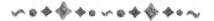

OUR LONDON STORY

Devina and I moved to London in 2014. We were instantly captivated by the city, and its vibrant and diverse restaurant scene. What was striking, however, was that despite knowing how much the English love their curries, we felt they were missing out on a huge part of what makes Indian food so special: the intricacy of flavours found in home-style dishes. We couldn't find anything like this on the market.

Thus, we sought to create a restaurant centred around incredible family recipes passed down from generation to generation, learnt at our mothers' feet. We all grew up surrounded by this and we've missed it since moving to London.

OUR RESTAURANT STORY

We opened Gunpowder, a home-style Indian kitchen, in 2015 at White's Row, Spitalfields. Taking residence in an old curry house, the restaurant is named after the spice mix 'gunpowder', a heady blend of pulses and spices, including chilli, curry leaves and *hing*, Hindi for asafoetida.

It's a happy coincidence that we are located close to Brick Lane, so famous for its curries, though it feels to us as if it has lost its soul. We wanted to bring something new and fresh to the scene, adding to the changing face of British curry, and bringing to it a sense of experimentation mixed with family tradition.

Since we opened, we have been delighted to find our 20-cover restaurant full at every lunch and dinner time, with people sometimes queuing in the street for a table. For us, the essence of Gunpowder is the smell of savoury spices mingling and the sound of friends laughing and talking as they gather to share plates of the food of our childhood.

SPICE GLOSSARY

ASAFOETIDA
Extracted from a plant of the giant fennel family, asafoetida is known for having a pungent smell but, by contrast, it adds a subtle flavour to dishes when cooked with other spices. It's a brilliant alternative to garlic and onions in dishes.

BLACK CARDAMOM
The pods of black cardamom are larger than the more-familiar green variety and they have a smoky character derived from the method of drying over open flames.

BLACK CUMIN (NIGELLA) SEEDS
Also known as nigella, black cumin is one the most revered medicinal seeds in history and it's one of the oldest spices known to be used. The tiny black seeds have a slightly bitter taste with some of the pungency of onion but also offer many other subtle nuances of flavour.

BLACK HORSE GRAMS
These small flattened lentils, multi-coloured in a spectrum that goes from beige to dark coffee brown, are one of the most protein-rich pulses on the planet. Historically, race horses were fed with this gram, hence its name.

BOONDI
These water droplet-sized, deep-fried crispy Indian snacks are made with chickpea flour and few spices. It's a main ingredient in making boondi raita and other snacks.

CAROM SEEDS
The use of carom seeds is mostly limited to India, in particular, Gujarat. The seeds have a thyme-like flavour and are traditionally used in roti and paratha.

CHAAT MASALA
Chaat is a generic name for hot, tangy, sweet nibbles but here it refers to a zingy, tangy, slightly hot spice blend. It gets its distinctive flavour from the black salt used to make it. Though often used as a spice in cooking, chaat masala is mostly used as a garnish on salads.

CHANA MASALA
This is a special blend of spices used to make a traditional chickpea curry. While every household will have their own unique recipe, many recipes feature asafoetida, nutmeg, ginger, cardamom, mango powder, cumin, fennel, black pepper, cloves, chilli, cinnamon, bay and fenugreek.

CLUSTER BEANS
The guar or cluster bean is a very valuable plant. Agriculturists in semi-arid regions of Rajasthan follow crop-rotation and grow these beans not only as a source of food, but also to replenish the soil before the next crop. In dishes, the beans offer a distinct flavour with a slightly bitter taste which works well with spices and rich sauces.

CURRY LEAVES
A staple of South Indian cooking, curry leaves are used in Indian and South East Asian cuisine in the same way as bay leaves are used in the West. The shiny, dark green, aromatic leaves are harvested from a tree in the citrus family. When fried in hot oil, curry leaves release a deliciously nutty aroma.

DEGGI MIRCH
Deggi mirch is a full-flavoured Indian spice that's milder than chilli powder but hotter than paprika. You can buy it in Indian grocers or online. Or, to make an easy substitute, mix 2 tablespoons paprika with 1 tablespoon chilli powder.

DRIED POMEGRANATE SEEDS
Also known as anardana, dried pomegranate seeds are sold in Indian as commonly as you would find sun-dried raisins or cranberries in the West. The seeds are often powdered to add a tangy, sour and sweet flavour to dishes and spice blends.

FENUGREEK
Both fenugreek leaves and seeds, known as methi in Hindi, are important ingredients in Indian cooking. They offer a subtle yet notable flavour that's somewhat like a cross between liquorice and fennel. Fenugreek is also hailed in ayurvedic medicine for its digestive and antioxidant benefits.

GARAM MASALA
The word garam refers to 'heating the body' in the Ayurvedic sense of the word. While the composition of garam masala differs regionally across the Indian subcontinent, each blend is believed to elevate body temperature.

GHEE
Ghee is a class of clarified butter that originated from the Indian subcontinent. It was historically made with butter made from water buffalo milk. Today, cow's milk butter is commonly used. As it's heated for longer, ghee has a stronger, nuttier, flavour and darker colour than standard clarified butter. Its higher burning point means that it's good for frying.

GUNPOWDER SPICE
Gunpowder is a traditional South Indian dry condiment made from roasted lentils, sesame seeds, curry leaves and other spices. It's traditionally used as a seasoning for idlis, rice or noodles.

JAGGERY
Jaggery is a completely unrefined sugar made from sugar cane juice or palm sap that is cooked down and set into blocks.

KASHMIR CHILLIES
With a vibrant red hue and very delicate heat, the Kashmiri chillies are used as much for their colour enriching properties as they are for their subtle, fruity chilli notes. Heat-wise, they're on the same level as Mexican poblano chillies.

KHUS
Khus is a dark green thick syrup made from the roots of khus grass (vetiver grass). It has a grassy, woody flavour that's often compared with that of lemongrass.

MADRAS CURRY POWDER
This is an aromatic blend of spices, often with a fair bit of heat, which is typical of the Madras region. The curry blend often features roasted and ground coriander, mustard, turmeric, black chickpeas, cumin, fenugreek, black pepper, garlic, fennel and salt.

MANGO GINGER
Also known as curcuma amada, mango ginger is a plant of the ginger family and is closely related to turmeric. It's traditionally used in pickles and chutneys.

MANGO POWDER
This is a fruity spice powder made from dried unripe green mangoes and is used as a citrusy seasoning. Also known as amchoor, it has a distinctive citrusy taste not too dissimilar to sumac, and is prized for offering the nutritional benefits of mangoes when the fresh fruit is out of season. It's a staple in many Indian spice blends.

MUSTARD OIL
This oil has a distinct mustard flavour and is the traditionally preferred oil for cooking in North and Eastern India.

NAGA CHILLIES
This is one of the hottest chilli peppers ever measured. It was briefly the 'World's Hottest Chilli' in 2011 according to the Guinness World Records with a rating of 1,382,118 Scoville units.

STONE FLOWER
Also known as black stone flower, this is a soft, dark lichen that gives the signature black hue to various masalas. It has a woody aroma and imparts a strong earthy flavour when cooked. It is widely used in Chettinad cuisine and, to some extent, in Hyderabadi and Marathi cuisines.

TAMARIND
Tamarind is a leguminous tree producing pod-like fruits containing an edible pulp with a distinct sweet and tangy flavour.

URAD DAL
Urad dal, also called urid dal, is made from hulled and split urad beans. This pale-yellow pulse doesn't require pre-soaking and is valued for its nutty flavour and creamy texture. It's the key ingredient used to make poppadoms, as well as as idli (steamed urad dal and rice cakes), dosa (thin, crisp-textured rice and lentil pancakes) and uttapam (sourdough pancakes).

YELLOW CHILLI POWDER
Compared to the fiery red chillies, yellow chillies are mild and mostly used to enhance the colour of dishes, as well as imparting a more subtle flavour. The yellow variety of chilli used to make this distinctive powder is mainly grown in Punjab and South Kashmir.

YELLOW MOONG
Yellow moong dal refers to moong beans that have been skinned and split, so that they're flat, yellow, and quick-cooking.

NOTE
Everyone has different tastes, so if you are sensitive to chilli or other spices, feel free to tweak and adjust the quantities in our recipes to suit your palate.

SMALL
PLATES

SMALL PLATES

When I was a child, my mother always had things in the fridge she could feed us for a snack or base a meal around. The following dishes are inspired by this. They are the nucleus of family food. The Chickpea Pancakes (see page 17) are a great example. You can make a large batch of batter, fry up some pancakes for breakfast and store the remaining mixture in the fridge so that you can whip up fresh hot pancakes on a whim. The Kale and Corn Cakes (see page 18) are another classic. We eat them for breakfast at home, but they make a great snack, or you can serve them with rice or even as a vegetarian burger.

You can also treat these dishes as Indian tapas or mezze of sorts, which, of course, is how we serve them in the restaurant. Enjoy our small plates as you wish and make them connect with your home and way of life.

SALLI PAR EEDU

SERVES 4

Parsees migrated from Greater Iran to Sindh and Gujarat, where they were given refuge, between the eighth and tenth centuries to avoid persecution following the Arab conquest of Persia. This migration brought the influence of Persian food to the local cuisine, this dish being a perfect example. It's like an Indian take on shakshuka.

1 litre sunflower or rapeseed oil, for frying
4 potatoes, peeled and julienned
2 tablespoons ghee
4 tomatoes, finely chopped
½ teaspoon freshly ground black pepper, plus extra to taste
½ teaspoon garam masala (shop-bought, or see page 161)
4 tablespoons freshly chopped coriander
4 medium eggs
bread, to serve
sea salt

1 Heat the oil in a deep frying pan over a high heat until it's sputtering, then deep-fry the julienned potatoes in small batches (about 1 handful for each batch) until the straws are crisp and golden. Remove with a slotted spoon and drain on kitchen paper, then sprinkle with a little salt and set aside.

2 Heat the ghee in a large frying pan with a lid. Add the chopped tomatoes, ½ teaspoon black pepper, the garam masala and a pinch of salt and cook for about 10 minutes until the tomatoes have broken down and thickened to a sauce. Add the fried potato straws and spread out to cover the base of the pan, pressing down gently with a spatula to create a thick layer.

3 Fold in half the chopped coriander, then make four little nests in the potato mix and crack an egg into each nest. Season the eggs with salt and pepper and cover with the lid.

4 Cook on a low heat for about 10 minutes until the eggs whites are fully set and the yolks are still runny. Scatter with the remaining coriander and serve straight away with your choice of bread.

NOTE

For a lighter dish, instead of deep-frying, toss the julienned potatoes with 2 tablespoons oil and roast in an oven preheated to 200°C/gas mark 6 for 40 minutes or until golden.

CHICKPEA PANCAKES

MAKES 12

This is one of my father's go-to breakfasts, which he'd happily eat every day. He likes the pancakes with chopped coriander, red onion and green chilli, but there are so many variations. Nirmal serves them with freshly grated coconut, or you can drizzle them with honey and serve with fruit. Alternatively, go savoury and match with fried eggs and one of the chutneys at the back of the book (see pages 184–186).

175g chickpea flour
75g plain white flour
50g cornflour
1 tablespoon soft brown sugar
½ teaspoon baking powder
½ teaspoon ground turmeric
150g natural yogurt
a pinch of sea salt
4 tablespoons grated fresh
    or desiccated coconut
1 thumb-sized piece of fresh ginger,
    peeled and finely chopped
1 green chilli, finely chopped
3–4 tablespoons butter or oil, for cooking

TO SERVE (OPTIONAL)
fried eggs
Tomato and Coriander Chutney (see
    page 186)

1 In a large bowl, combine the flours, brown sugar, baking powder and turmeric. In another bowl, whisk the yogurt, salt and 150ml water together, then stir into the dry ingredients until the batter is smooth and the consistency of double cream.

2 Mix the coconut, ginger and chilli in a separate bowl and have at the ready.

3 Place a large frying pan over a medium heat. Add 1–2 teaspoons of the butter or oil and, when hot, add a ladle (2–3 tablespoons) of batter, then swirl the pan to achieve a thin and even layer. Sprinkle a good pinch of the coconut mix over the surface of the pancake and cook for 2–3 minutes or until bubbles form on the top and the edges shrink from the sides of the pan. Flip the pancake and cook for a further minute or until both sides are golden brown. Remove from the pan and keep warm while you make the next pancake. Continue in this way until you've used up all the batter – you can freeze any surplus pancakes or batter for up to 6 months.

4 Serve warm with fried eggs and Tomato and Coriander Chutney, or the topping of your choice.

KALE AND CORN CAKES

This is the sort of dish you'd find in school canteens back home in India. I used to love these as a kid. In fact, I still do. I love eating them with the spicy heat of mustard dolloped on the side. They also work well with ketchup or, as Nirmal suggests, a raita.

2 tablespoons rapeseed or olive oil,
  plus extra for shallow-frying
1 green chilli, finely chopped
1 tablespoon grated fresh ginger
100g kale, washed, dried and finely chopped
100g fresh or tinned sweetcorn kernels,
  drained
½ teaspoon smoked paprika
½ teaspoon garam masala (shop-bought,
  or see page 161)
¼ teaspoon cumin seeds
200g boiled potatoes, coarsely grated
80g panko breadcrumbs
4 tablespoons freshly chopped coriander
sea salt, to taste
raita or chutney, to serve

1 Place a large non-stick frying pan over a high heat. Swirl the oil around the pan, then add the chilli, ginger and kale and cook until the kale starts to wilt down – about 5 minutes.

2 Fold in the sweetcorn and spices and cook for a further 2–3 minutes, then take off the heat. Add the grated potato, panko breadcrumbs and fresh coriander. Season with salt, to taste, and mix well until everything comes together. Set aside and leave to cool.

3 Once cooled, divide the mixture into 12–15 golf ball-sized nuggets and roll each ball between your palms until smooth, then gently press to flatten a little into a disc.

4 Place the pan back on a high heat and add the oil for shallow-frying. When hot, cook the kale and corn cakes in small batches until golden on each side and then transfer to a kitchen paper-lined plate. Serve hot with any raita or tangy chutney.

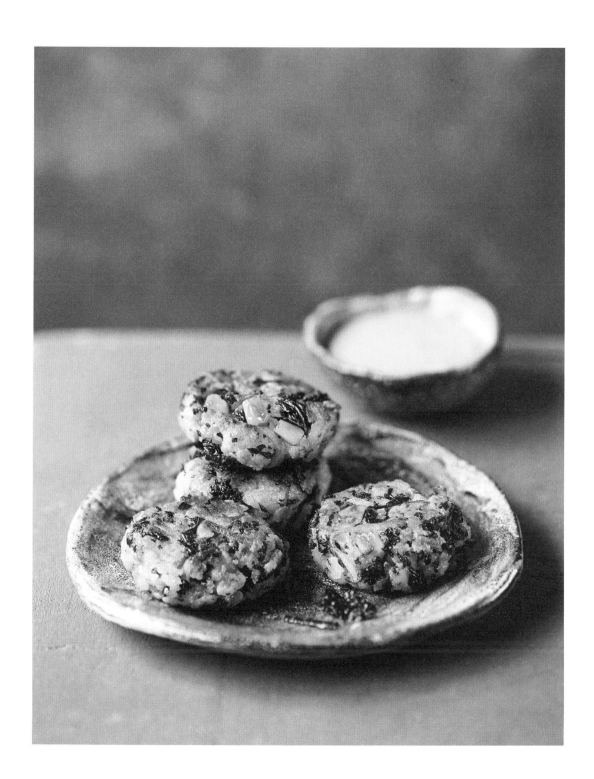

MARKET-STYLE SCRAMBLED EGGS

SERVES 4

In Indian markets, the vendors cook everything on smoking hot plates. The heat is so intense that you can't achieve the wonderful creamy texture you get when you scramble eggs over controlled heat at home. To counteract this, they add onion, tomato and, of course, lots of herbs and spices, which keeps the eggs moist and delicious. It's a true taste of Indian street food. I love these eggs for breakfast, but they're great anytime.

12 medium eggs
2 tablespoons ghee
6 curry leaves (fresh or dried)
1 teaspoon cumin seeds
½ teaspoon yellow mustard seeds
1 onion, finely chopped
1 thumb-sized piece of fresh ginger, peeled and finely chopped
1 green chilli, finely chopped
2 tomatoes, finely chopped
30g fresh coriander, chopped
1 tablespoon butter, plus extra to finish
1 teaspoon ground turmeric
a pinch of chilli powder
a pinch of asafoetida (optional)
4 tablespoons finely chopped chives
grilled sourdough bread, to serve
sea salt

1 In a large bowl, whisk the eggs together and set aside.

2 Place a large pan over a medium heat. Add the ghee and, once melted, tip in the curry leaves, cumin and mustard seeds, onion, ginger and green chilli. Sauté for 3–4 minutes. Add the tomatoes, fold through half the chopped coriander and cook for 2 minutes.

3 Add the butter, turmeric, chilli powder, asafoetida (if using) and a good pinch of sea salt or more, to taste, and stir to mix well. Pour in the beaten eggs and keep whisking until they are cooked.

4 Add a little extra butter, if you like, and sprinkle with the remaining chopped coriander leaves and the chives. Serve with grilled and buttered white sourdough bread.

BEEF GUJIYA

MAKES 12–15

My father and a lot of men his age like to keep fit, so they go out in the morning for a long walk or run. However, once they've finished with all that exercise, they can't resist the temptation of tucking into one of these classic street food pastries. The classic preparation is to deep-fry them, and, of course, they're delicious that way. But if you're more health conscious, you can shallow fry or bake them instead and they'll still taste wonderful.

FOR THE PASTRY
400g baby leaf spinach, washed
1 tablespoon dried fenugreek leaves
   or seeds, ground to a powder
5 tablespoons ghee
500g plain flour
100g fine semolina
2 teaspoons caster sugar
1 teaspoon sea salt
5 tablespoons rapeseed or olive oil
1 litre sunflower or rapeseed oil, for frying

FOR THE FILLING
500g minced beef
2 tablespoons natural or Greek yogurt
1 teaspoon ground turmeric
4 garlic cloves, very finely chopped
1 teaspoon cumin seeds
seeds from 3 green cardamom pods
seeds from 1 black cardamom pod
4 cloves
½ cinnamon stick
6 black peppercorns
2 tablespoons rapeseed or olive oil
2 onions, finely chopped
1 tablespoon grated fresh ginger
1 green chilli, finely chopped
a pinch of chilli powder
1 tablespoon ground coriander
1 large tomato, finely chopped
4 tablespoons freshly chopped coriander

FOR THE PASTRY

1 Place a frying pan with a lid over a high heat, add the spinach and fenugreek and cover. Take off the heat immediately and set aside to let the spinach wilt down.

2 Transfer the wilted spinach to a sieve and squeeze to remove any excess liquid, then purée in a blender with 1 tablespoon of the ghee. Set aside.

3 Sift the flour into a bowl. Add the semolina, sugar and salt and stir to mix. Add the remaining ghee and the oil and, using your fingers, mix well to incorporate so that the mixture takes the form of breadcrumbs and binds to a certain extent.

4 Add the spinach mixture and mix again with your hands, kneading lightly. If the dough is too dry, add 1–2 tablespoons water, just enough to bring it together into a soft but tight pastry dough. If it's too wet, add a little more flour. Set aside, covered with a damp cloth, for 20 minutes.

FOR THE FILLING

5 In a bowl, mix together the beef, yogurt, turmeric and garlic, then leave to marinate in the fridge for 30 minutes–1 hour.

6 Place a large frying pan over a medium heat. Add the cumin seeds, green and black cardamom seeds, cloves, cinnamon and black peppercorns and toast for 1–2 minutes or until fragrant. Transfer to a spice or coffee grinder or pestle and mortar and grind to a powder. Set aside.

7 Place the pan back on the heat. Add the oil and, once hot, sauté the onions until golden. Stir in the ground spice mix, the ginger, green chilli, chilli powder and ground coriander and cook for a minute, then fold in the tomato. Cook for 5–10 minutes or until it has broken down into a thick paste.

8 Stir the marinated beef mince into the pan and cook on a medium heat for 15 minutes or until the mince is just golden. Fold the chopped coriander through and set aside to cool slightly.

TO ASSEMBLE THE PASTRIES

9 Divide the dough into 12–15 small balls and, using a rolling pin, roll out each ball into a 10cm-diameter circle.

10 Fill half the circle with the beef mixture (about a tablespoon), leaving space around the edges. Moisten the edges of the pastry with a little water, then fold the pastry over and seal the filling in by curling the edges inwards, like a Cornish pasty. Take care that the filling does not ooze out. Prepare all the gujiyas in the same way and spread out on a clean tea towel.

11 Heat the oil in a deep frying pan over a high heat until it's sputtering. Reduce the heat a little and deep-fry the pastries, in small batches, for about 5 minutes until golden. Make sure each pastry has plenty of space in the frying pan. Once cooked, transfer to a kitchen paper-lined tray. Serve immediately or gently warm further in an oven preheated to 180°C/gas mark 4 for 10 minutes.

NOTE

Gujiya moulds can also be used – they are easily available. Place the rolled-out dough in a greased gujiya mould and add a tablespoon of filling mixture on one side. Moisten the edges and fold one side of the mould over the other. Trim the excess edges and reuse.

ALOO GUJIYA

MAKES 12–15

This is the vegetarian spin on gujiya – and it's just as if not more delicious than its meaty counterpart (see page 22). The spinach gives the pastry a vibrant green hue.

FOR THE PASTRY
400g baby leaf spinach, rinsed
  and drained
1 tablespoon dried fenugreek leaves
  or seeds, ground to a powder
5 tablespoons ghee
500g plain flour, plus extra
  if needed
100g fine semolina
2 teaspoons caster sugar
1 teaspoon sea salt
5 tablespoons rapeseed or olive oil
1 litre sunflower or rapeseed oil,
  for frying

FOR THE FILLING
2 tablespoons rapeseed or olive oil
2 bay leaves
1 teaspoon cumin seeds
2 large onions, finely chopped
2 tablespoons grated fresh ginger
2 garlic cloves, finely chopped
½ teaspoon sea salt
1 teaspoon freshly ground
  black pepper
a pinch of chilli powder
1kg new potatoes, boiled
  and peeled
2 tablespoons freshly squeezed
  lime juice
2 teaspoons ground cumin (see Tip)
30g coriander leaves, finely chopped

FOR THE PASTRY
1 Place a frying pan with a lid over a high heat, add the spinach and fenugreek and cover. Take off the heat immediately and set aside to let the spinach wilt down.

2 Transfer the wilted spinach to a sieve and squeeze to remove any excess liquid, then purée in a blender with 1 tablespoon of the ghee. Set aside.

3 Sift the flour into a bowl. Add the semolina, sugar and salt and stir to mix. Add the remaining ghee and the 5 tablespoons oil and, using your fingers, mix well to incorporate so that the mixture takes the form of breadcrumbs and binds to a certain extent.

4 Add the spinach mixture and mix again with your hands, kneading lightly. If the dough is too dry, add 1–2 tablespoons water, just enough to bring it together into a soft pastry dough. If it's too wet, add a little more flour. Set the dough aside, covered with a damp cloth, for 20 minutes.

FOR THE FILLING
5 Place a frying pan over a high heat. Add the oil, reduce the heat to medium and add the bay leaves and cumin seeds. Wait for the cumin seeds to sputter, then fold in the onions, ginger and garlic and gently fry for 10 minutes until the onions turn golden brown. Add the salt, black pepper and chilli powder and cook for 2–3 minutes until the oil separates from the mixture.

6 Tip the potatoes into the pan and stir to coat in all the spices, crushing and mashing them as you mix them through. Add the lime juice and 100ml water to moisten the mix and boil just enough so that the spice mixture is absorbed by the potatoes, but not so much that they break up.

7 Sprinkle with roasted ground cumin and the chopped coriander leaves, then set aside to cool down. Once the mixture is cool, mash a little more to give you a smooth filling.

TIP

For maximum flavour, dry-roast whole cumin seeds for 1–2 minutes or until fragrant, and grind in a spice or coffee grinder or a pestle and mortar, to make your own roasted ground cumin. The difference in flavour compared to shop-bought ground cumin is remarkable.

TO ASSEMBLE THE PASTRIES

8 Divide the dough into 12–15 small balls and, using a rolling pin, roll out each ball of dough into a 10cm-diameter circle.

9 Fill half the circle with the aloo mixture (about a tablespoon), leaving space around the edges. Moisten the edges of the pastry with a little water, then fold the pastry over and seal the filling in by curling the edges inwards, like a Cornish pasty. Take care that the filling does not ooze out. Prepare all the gujiyas in the same way and spread out on a clean tea towel.

10 Heat the oil in a deep frying pan over a high heat until it's sputtering. Reduce the heat a little and deep-fry the pastries, in small batches, for about 5 minutes until golden. Make sure each pastry has plenty of space in the frying pan. Once cooked, transfer to a kitchen paper-lined tray. Serve immediately or gently warm further in an oven preheated to 180°C/gas mark 4 for 10 minutes.

NOTE

Gujiya moulds can also be used – see note on page 23.

LAMB KIDNEY AND CHICKEN LIVER ON TOAST

SERVES 4

This is another of my dad's best-loved dishes. In India, we waste nothing. Instead of buying just the chicken breast or thigh, we buy the whole chicken. The same thing applies to lamb – we don't want just the shank or the cutlet. It has to be sustainable and affordable at the same time. This means we have all the extras to use up and this is one of our favourite ways of cooking the livers and kidneys.

4 tablespoons rapeseed oil or butter
2 onions, thinly sliced
4 garlic cloves, very finely chopped
8 curry leaves (fresh are best if you can get them, but dried are fine)
2 teaspoons garam masala (shop-bought, or see page 161)
1 teaspoon ground turmeric
¼ teaspoon chilli powder
4 cloves, finely ground
4 tablespoons tomato purée
200g trimmed chicken livers
200g cored lamb kidney
sea salt

TO SERVE
freshly chopped coriander or micro herbs (such as radishes or baby mustard leaves)
grilled sourdough bread

1 Heat the oil or butter in a large frying pan over a medium heat, add the onions and a pinch of salt and cook for 5–10 minutes or until soft and a little golden.

2 Add the garlic and curry leaves and cook for 30 seconds, then stir in the garam masala, turmeric, chilli powder and cloves. Add the tomato purée and fry for about 5 minutes until oil is released and it turns brown.

3 Add the chicken livers and kidney and pour in 200ml water. Stir well once, then cover and simmer over a low heat for 10 minutes.

4 Remove the lid, stir again and check the thickness of the gravy, adding a little more water if needed. Season with salt, to taste, then serve on grilled sourdough with fresh coriander or micro herbs scattered on top.

TIP

For best results, once cooked, leave to cool, then cover and refrigerate this dish for 6 hours or overnight, as then the liver and kidney absorb all the oil and masala flavour. Gently reheat, adding a little more water if necessary. Add extra curry leaves if you don't like the aroma/taste of fresh cooked liver and kidney.

PORZI OKRA

SERVES 4

This recipe has South Indian roots, where bindi or okra is very popular. This is the sort of thing Indian mothers make to get their children to eat green vegetables.

500g okra, cut into 4 lengthways
1½ tablespoons freshly squeezed lemon juice
150g chickpea flour
1 tablespoon mango powder
1 tablespoon chilli powder
½ teaspoon Gunpowder Spice Mix
  (see page 158)
20 curry leaves (fresh are best if you can
  get them, but dried are fine), toasted and
  ground to a powder
1 litre sunflower oil, for deep-frying
1 tablespoon chaat masala
sea salt

1 In a bowl, mix the okra with the lemon juice and set aside. In a separate large bowl, mix the chickpea flour with the mango powder, chilli powder, gunpowder spice mix and powdered curry leaves and a good pinch of salt. In small batches, coat the okra in the seasoned chickpea flour.

2 Pour the oil into a deep, heavy-based pan suitable for deep-frying and set over a high heat until sputtering. Check that the oil is hot enough by adding one piece of coated okra – it should rise to the top and crisp within 1–2 minutes.

3 When your oil is hot enough, fry the coated okra in small batches for 3 minutes until crisp and golden. Remove with a slotted spoon and drain on kitchen paper. Continue until all the okra is cooked, then serve immediately with a sprinkling of chaat masala and a dusting of salt on top.

SAVOURY
FRENCH TOAST

SERVES 4

When I was little, we used to watch a lot of American TV programmes like *The Wonder Years*. We became so curious about American food through these shows. My mother created this dish to cater to our curiosity. Of course, she's given it an Indian twist.

3 medium eggs
¼ teaspoon ground turmeric
3 tablespoons milk
1 green chilli, very finely chopped
½ teaspoon grated fresh ginger
1 garlic clove, very finely chopped
2 tablespoons freshly chopped coriander
1 tablespoon finely chopped spring onion
1 cherry tomato, finely chopped
4 thick slices of brioche, sliced on
    the diagonal
2–3 tablespoons butter, for cooking
sea salt and freshly ground black pepper
Tomato and Coriander Chutney (see page
    186), to serve

1 In a shallow dish, whisk the eggs with the turmeric and milk, then add the chilli, ginger, garlic, coriander, spring onion and tomato. Season with a good pinch of salt and black pepper.

2 Dip the bread in the egg mixture, one piece at a time, and leave to soak for 15–30 seconds on each side or until nicely coated. Let any excess mixture drip off the bread, then set aside.

3 Melt 1 tablespoon of the butter in a non-stick frying pan set over a medium heat and, in batches, fry each piece of eggy bread on both sides for 2–3 minutes until golden brown.

4 Work quickly and serve immediately with homemade Tomato and Coriander Chutney.

MUSTARD BROCCOLI

MAKHANI SAUCE

SERVES 2 AS A MAIN, 4 AS A STARTER OR SIDE

MAKES 250ML

We use mustard a lot in the east of India and here we pair it with broccoli, which is in the same family. In India, you often see this dish made with cauliflower, so you could easily interchange them. We prefer broccoli for the restaurant, as it really soaks in all the flavours and gets even crisper when flashed under the grill. It's one of the most popular vegetarian dishes at Gunpowder. We think it'll become a favourite in your home, too. *Photographed overleaf.*

1 head of broccoli, halved
100g Greek yogurt
50g full-fat cream cheese
2 tablespoons wholegrain mustard
½ teaspoon chilli powder
1 teaspoon chaat masala
1 teaspoon ground turmeric
½ teaspoon ground coriander
¼ teaspoon ground cumin
2 tablespoons mustard or rapeseed oil, plus 1 teaspoon
1 tablespoon chickpea flour
2–3 tablespoons ghee, melted
sea salt
Makhani Sauce (see right) and pickled beetroot, to serve

1 Bring a pan of salted water to the boil and cook the broccoli for 3 minutes, then drain and rinse under ice-cold water to prevent it from cooking further. Shake off any excess water and set aside.

2 In a large dish, mix together the yogurt, cream cheese, mustard, chilli powder, chaat masala, turmeric, coriander, cumin and the 2 tablespoons of mustard or rapeseed oil.

3 Set a frying pan over a medium heat and toast the chickpea flour for 30 seconds. Add the remaining 1 teaspoon of oil, mix, and toast for a further 30 seconds, making a fragrant paste. Whisk this into the yogurt mix, then thoroughly coat the broccoli in the creamy spice paste and set aside to marinate for 30 minutes.

4 Set your oven grill to high and grill the broccoli, cut-side down, for 10–15 minutes, basting it with the melted ghee. When golden on top, turn over and grill 5 minutes on the other side, or until nicely coloured.

5 Serve on a base of Makhani Sauce with pickled beetroot sprinkled on top.

Although here we are serving it with our famous Mustard Broccoli, this sauce is also a lovely accompaniment to our Kale and Corn Cakes (see page 18) or any grilled meat, especially lamb.

2 tablespoons unsalted butter
2 garlic cloves, very finely chopped
2 teaspoons grated fresh ginger
500g tomatoes, diced
½ teaspoon ground fenugreek seeds
½ teaspoon cumin seeds
3 cloves
3 green cardamom pods
¼ teaspoon freshly ground black pepper
a pinch of chilli powder
¼ teaspoon freshly grated nutmeg
2–3 tablespoons double cream
1 teaspoon honey, or to taste (optional)
sea salt

1 Set a frying pan over a high heat and add 1 tablespoon of the butter. Once melted, add the garlic, ginger and a pinch of salt and cook for a minute.

2 Fold the tomatoes and all the spices through. Cook over a medium heat for 5–10 minutes until the tomatoes have broken down and darkened in a colour a little.

3 Spoon the mixture into a food processor or blender and blend until fairly smooth. Press through a sieve, giving you a smooth sauce. Warm the sauce gently in a saucepan with the remaining tablespoon of butter. Once the butter is melted, swirl in the cream.

4 Let the sauce gently bubble away over medium-low heat for about 5 minutes until it has thickened and darkened further. Season with salt and the honey, if needed, to taste. Serve warm.

AUBERGINE BHARTA

Nobody, and I mean nobody, makes this dish like my mother and my grandmother. We joke that you must have the surname Baweja to make this dish well, but here we've given away our family secret. Two extra tips to make this dish a hit. First, mash the aubergine with a fork rather than chopping it with a knife. Second, use the core of the aubergine – this part has the most flavour but for some reason people tend to throw it away – and don't be afraid to keep a few bits of the burnt skin, too.

1 large (800g) or 2 small (400g) aubergines
½ teaspoon rapeseed or olive oil
1 tablespoon ghee
1 teaspoon cumin seeds
2 medium-sized onions, thinly sliced
1½ teaspoons grated fresh ginger
1 garlic clove, finely chopped
½ green chilli, finely chopped
1 large or 2 medium tomatoes, finely diced
½ teaspoon ground turmeric
1 tablespoon ground cumin
1 tablespoon ground coriander
½ tablespoon garam masala (shop-bought, or see page 161)
2 tablespoons freshly chopped coriander
sea salt

1 Rub the aubergine(s) with the oil and roast for about 15 minutes over an open flame on the hob until charred all over and tender right the way through, turning often. You can finish it off in an oven preheated to 200°C/gas mark 6 if it's nicely charred but not tender enough. Set aside to cool.

2 Strip the aubergine of its charred skin – it should come off easily with your hands or when scraped with a spoon. Discard the skin and mash the pulp thoroughly, then set aside.

3 Place the ghee in a pan over a medium heat and add the cumin seeds. When they crackle, add the onions and gently cook for about 1 minute until golden brown. Add the ginger, garlic and green chilli and sauté for a few more seconds. Stir in the tomato, turmeric, cumin and ground coriander and cook for a further minute, then fold in the mashed aubergine and garam masala and cook for 3–4 minutes.

4 Season with sea salt, to taste, and serve warm with the chopped fresh coriander scattered on top.

GUNPOWDER

PLEASE WAIT
TO BE
SEATED

THANK YOU

GUNPOWDER ALOO CHAAT

This dish reminds me of my winter holidays. We'd go to Delhi and this would be the first dish we'd eat in the markets. Every region of India has their own version. In this one, the potatoes are fried, which gives them a wonderful crust. The vendors in the markets make them with so much theatre, flattening the hot, boiled potatoes before smashing them into the pan of sizzling ghee. Ah, the aroma when they are cooking is amazing. In the east, aloo chaat is made with boiled potatoes but it really can't compete with this.

FOR THE GUNPOWDER ALOO
20 baby new potatoes, washed
150ml sunflower or rapeseed oil, for frying
1–2 tablespoons Gunpowder Spice Mix
  (see page 158)

FOR THE SWEET YOGURT
200g Greek yogurt
1 teaspoon caster sugar

FOR THE SPICED TAMARIND AND DATE
CHUTNEY
50g tamarind paste
50g pitted dates
50g jaggery or brown sugar
¼ teaspoon ground cumin
¼ teaspoon ground coriander
½ teaspoon grated fresh ginger
a pinch of chilli powder
sea salt, to taste

FOR THE BLACK HORSE GRAM SALAD
200g cooked black horse gram beans
  (see page 10) or Puy lentils
2 tomatoes, finely chopped
1 red onion, finely chopped
1 green chilli, or more or less, to taste
½ teaspoon black salt
1 teaspoon mango powder

TO GARNISH
4 thin rounds of peeled fresh lotus root
micro coriander leaves

1 Boil the baby potatoes in salted water for 25 minutes or until tender right the way through. Drain, cool and then gently press each potato flat so that it looks like a little potato cake. Set aside.

2 In a bowl, mix together the yogurt and sugar and set aside.

3 Place the tamarind, dates and 250ml water in a blender and purée until smooth. Transfer this mixture to a saucepan and simmer until warmed through, then add the jaggery or brown sugar and spices, season with salt, and cook over a medium heat for 5–10 minutes until it darkens and thickens to the consistency of ketchup. Strain through a sieve and set aside.

4 In a large bowl, toss all the salad ingredients together.

5 In a large frying pan, heat the oil over a high heat and fry the potato cakes for about 3–4 minutes until golden and crisp on both sides. Fry the lotus root rounds in the same oil for 1 minute until golden and crisp, then remove and drain on kitchen paper.

6 Divide the fried potatoes between serving plates and top each plate with 2 tablespoons of the black horse gram salad, followed by a sprinkling of gunpowder spice. Top with a drizzle of the sweet yogurt and tamarind chutney, followed by a small spoon of salad. Garnish with a lotus root crisp and a scattering of micro coriander leaves.

CHENNA PATURI

Chenna paturi is a traditional dish of paneer that's rubbed with a punchy paste made with mustard, coconut and green chillies. This is a vegetarian adaption of the popular Bengali fish recipe paturi (see page 107), one of the royal dishes of Bengali cuisine. Sometimes large pumpkin leaves are used in place of banana leaves. You can make this with either.

600g paneer, cut into 4 even pieces
250g wholegrain mustard
2 tablespoons mustard oil or rapeseed oil
4 tablespoons lemon juice
4 tablespoons freshly grated or
  dessicated coconut
2 tablespoons grated fresh ginger
4 garlic cloves, finely minced
1 green chilli, finely chopped
1 teaspoon Kashmiri chilli powder (see Tip)
2 tablespoons ground turmeric
1 vegetable stock cube
4 x 23cm square pieces of banana leaf

1 Take a bowl and mix the mustard, oil, lemon juice, coconut, ginger, garlic, green chilli, chilli powder, turmeric and stock cube to a make a coarse paste.

2 Add the paneer pieces and mix until evenly coated. Cover and keep them in the fridge for 2–3 hours to marinate.

3 Gently warm the banana leaves over an open flame for 10-20 seconds on both sides, ensuring they don't get burnt.

4 Place a piece of marinated paneer in the middle of each banana leaf square and fold the leaf around it, making an envelope (you can tie the envelope with string).

5 Set the paneer parcels in a steamer basket and steam for 25 minutes. Alternatively, you can place them in a warm, lidded frying pan with 2 tablespoons water and steam through that way.

6 Once the paneer is steamed, remove from steamer and keep aside. Set a large, dry frying or griddle pan over a high heat. Grill each paneer parcel for 2 minutes on each side until it is marked by the grill. Serve hot.

TIP

Kashmiri chilli powder can be made by grinding whole dried Kashmiri chillies to a powder. Alternatively, use half the amount (or less) or normal chilli powder, as Kashmiri chillies are quite mild and fruity in comparison.

BULGUR MOONG SALAD

SERVES 2–4

This recipe is from Nirmal's family. It's made with lighter, cheaper ingredients from his village and is a good way to balance lots of heavy dishes.

FOR THE SALAD
100g bulgur wheat, soaked overnight in
    enough fresh water to fully cover
100g yellow moong dal, soaked overnight in
    enough fresh water to fully cover
1 tablespoon grated fresh ginger
2 spring onions, finely chopped
1 tomato, deseeded and finely diced
juice of 1 lime
sea salt, to taste

FOR THE DRESSING
4 tablespoons olive or rapeseed oil
2 garlic cloves, very finely chopped
8 mint leaves, finely chopped

1 First make the dressing. Heat the oil in a frying pan until just smoking, then take it off the heat. Set aside to cool a little, then add the garlic. When the oil is completely cooled, add the chopped mint and set aside to infuse for 2 hours. Strain into a jug and reserve until ready to use.

2 Drain the bulgur wheat and moong dal and rinse with fresh water, then transfer to a large bowl.

3 Add all the remaining salad ingredients and mix together. Season with salt, to taste. Toss with the dressing and serve.

CHUTNEY CHEESE SANDWICH

SERVES 4

My family are members of a huge golf club in India. In fact, it's the largest golf club outside the UK. When we go, we play golf all day and the loser has to buy the others breakfast. We used to get these bland toasted cheese sandwiches at the club and I would always complain, so the chef added this wonderful fresh chutney, and BOOM – it was a whole new dish! I could eat this every day.

5–6 tablespoons butter
¼ green pepper, finely chopped
¼ red pepper, finely chopped
¼ red onion, finely chopped
100g mild Cheddar cheese, grated
200g mozzarella cheese, torn
a pinch of chilli powder
8 thick slices of bread

FOR THE MINT AND CORIANDER CHUTNEY
30g mint, finely chopped
15g coriander, finely chopped
50g grated fresh coconut (see Note on
    page 51)
1 green chilli, finely chopped
2 teaspoons cumin seeds, toasted
50ml freshly squeezed lime juice
a pinch of ground ginger or
    ¼ teaspoon grated fresh ginger
sea salt, to taste

1 In a bowl, mix together all the ingredients for the mint and coriander chutney and then set aside.

2 Heat 1 tablespoon of the butter in a non-stick sauté pan, add the peppers and onion and sauté for 5 minutes or until tender. Remove from the heat and transfer to a bowl. Add the cheeses, chilli powder and half of the chutney. Mix well.

3 Use the remaining butter to lightly butter one side of each of the bread slices and pile the cheese mix on four of the slices. Cover with the remaining bread to make four sandwiches.

4 Heat a sandwich toaster or set a large frying pan over a high heat. Add a generous slick of butter to the sandwich toaster or the frying pan and toast the sandwiches until golden on each side, adding more butter, if necessary.

5 Serve hot with the remaining mint and coriander chutney on the side.

KADAI PANEER PARCEL

SERVES 4–6

In every Indian bakery you can see items that are clearly inspired by French pâtissiers, but of course there's always an Indian twist. This is a classic example. You've got all that wonderful, buttery, flaky pastry, yet housed inside is Indian cheese and fragrant spices.

325g ready-rolled puff pastry,
   fully defrosted if frozen
1 teaspoon rapeseed or olive oil
1 onion, finely chopped
1 teaspoon grated fresh ginger
1 garlic clove, very finely chopped
1 red pepper, finely diced
1 green pepper, finely diced
400g paneer, diced
¼ teaspoon ground cumin
½ teaspoon ground coriander
½ teaspoon ground turmeric
½ teaspoon chaat masala
¼ teaspoon mango powder
a pinch of chilli powder or chilli flakes
4 tablespoons freshly chopped coriander
sea salt

1 Preheat the oven to 200°C/gas mark 6. Line a baking sheet with greaseproof paper.

2 Set a frying pan over a medium heat. Add the oil and swirl in the onion. Cook for 10 minutes or until tender and a little golden.

3 Stir in the ginger and garlic, then add the peppers and a little salt. Mix well, cover and cook for 2–3 minutes until the peppers are tender.

4 Take off the heat. Fold in the paneer, all the spices and the chopped coriander. Mix well.

5 Unroll the pastry sheets. Put all the stuffing in the centre and fold the pastry over the filling lengthways, so that you have a long, thin rectangular package.

6 Use a fork to gently, but firmly, press into the edges to help seal. Cut into 5cm portions.

7 Arrange the parcels on the prepared baking sheet. Bake for 15 minutes or until golden and puffed up. Transfer to a cooling rack to rest for 5 minutes before serving. These are delicious served with the Makhani Sauce (see page 31) and crispy kale – this is how we serve it in the restaurant.

TIPS
Use any vegetable and spice combination for the parcels. It is very important to leave them to cool for 5 minutes – this will make the puffs nice and flaky AND they won't burn your mouth. If you don't have a cooling rack, improvise – prop an oven rack above the work surface and use that.

PUNJABI CHANA MASALA

SERVES 4

I'm Punjabi and every good Punjabi boy loves chana masala. It's an easy vegetable dish, and pure comfort food. Serve with rice, raita or chutney, and a salad.

4 tablespoons rapeseed or olive oil
1 tablespoon grated fresh ginger
1–2 green chillies, finely chopped
ground seeds from 3 black cardamom pods
½ cinnamon stick
2 onions, finely chopped
4 garlic cloves, very finely chopped
2 tomatoes, finely chopped
2 teaspoons ground coriander
1½ teaspoons garam masala (shop-bought, or see page 161)
½ teaspoon chilli powder, to taste
4 teaspoons Chana Masala (see page 10)
600g cooked chickpeas, drained and rinsed
1 teaspoon dried fenugreek leaves
4 tablespoons freshly chopped coriander
bread, to serve
sea salt

1 Heat the oil in a deep non-stick pan over a medium heat, add the ginger, green chillies, ground cardamom and cinnamon stick and cook, stirring, for 30 seconds.

2 Add the onions and garlic and sauté for 5 minutes until the onions are soft and a little golden. Add the chopped tomatoes, mix well and cook for 3 minutes, stirring occasionally. Fold the ground coriander, garam masala, chilli powder and chana masala into the vegetables and cook for a further minute, stirring occasionally.

3 Add the chickpeas, fenugreek, 400ml water and a pinch of salt. Stir everything together and cook on a medium heat, stirring occasionally, for 15–20 minutes or until the water dries out.

4 Serve warm, scattered with the chopped fresh coriander and your choice of bread.

TANDOORI PANEER AND SAAG

SERVES 2–4

These are two staple dishes in my family. In my house, we would either have the spinach sauce, which we call *saag*, or the tandoori paneer, but they were never served together. They do, however, make the perfect marriage, so I'm happy to unite them here.

FOR THE TANDOORI PANEER
2 teaspoons chickpea flour
1 teaspoon mustard or rapeseed oil
½ teaspoon freshly squeezed
    lemon juice
150g Greek or natural yogurt
1 teaspoon grated fresh ginger
2 garlic cloves, very finely chopped
1 green chilli, finely chopped
a pinch of chilli powder
½ teaspoon black cumin seeds
½ teaspoon carom seeds
1 teaspoon ground turmeric
2 teaspoons chaat masala
1 teaspoon dried fenugreek leaves
2 tablespoons finely
    chopped coriander
500g paneer, cut into 3cm cubes
chilli flakes, to serve
sea salt

FOR THE SAAG
1kg baby leaf spinach, washed
    and drained
4 tablespoons rapeseed or olive oil
2 teaspoons cumin seeds
2 dried red chillies
2 onions, finely chopped
6 garlic cloves, finely chopped
1 thumb-sized piece of fresh ginger,
    peeled and julienned
1 green chilli, finely chopped
½ teaspoon ground turmeric
2 tablespoons freshly grated tomato
2 teaspoons Malvani Garam Masala
    (see page 161)
1 teaspoon mango powder (optional)
3 tablespoons single cream
2 tablespoons butter
sea salt, to taste

1 For the tandoori paneer, place a frying pan over a medium heat. Add the chickpea flour and toast for 30 seconds, then take off the heat and fold in the oil and lemon juice to make a paste. Stir in the yogurt and all the remaining ingredients, apart from the paneer, salt and chilli flakes. Mix everything together, then add the paneer and coat thoroughly in the mix. Dust with a sprinkling of salt and set aside to marinate for 1 hour.

2 For the saag, blanch the spinach in a pan of boiling water, then drain, refresh with cold water and set aside to cool. Transfer to a blender and blend until smooth, then set aside.

3 Preheat your grill to high.

4 Meanwhile, heat the oil in a frying pan over a medium heat. Add the cumin seeds and dried chillies and stir through the oil for 30 seconds, then add the onions and cook for 5–10 minutes or until soft and glossy.

5 Add the garlic, ginger, green chilli and turmeric and sauté for a minute, then fold in the tomato pulp and cook down for 1–2 minutes until the tomato has thickened to a paste.

6 Add the garam masala, mango powder (if using), cream and butter and, as soon as the butter is melted, fold through the spinach, then take off the heat and set aside.

7 Arrange the marinated paneer on a grill pan and flash under the hot grill, cooking for 3 minutes on each side or until lightly charred all over. Alternatively, you can heat a little oil in a non-stick pan and fry the paneer over a medium heat.

8 Gently warm the saag through before serving, then spoon a little into the bottom of each serving bowl and top with the grilled paneer. A shaking of chilli flakes finishes this dish off to perfection.

CORIANDER-SPICED ROAST VEG SALAD
with WALNUTS

SERVES 4

My mother is a vegetarian and like any good mother she was always trying to get more vegetables into our diet. She used to roast up great big trays of vegetables sprinkled with fragrant spices. This was her way of enticing us, and it worked. Nirmal has dressed this up a bit further with the walnuts and the dressing. It's a great dish for the whole family.

½ butternut squash, peeled, deseeded
   and cut into 3cm pieces
1 courgette, chopped into 3cm pieces
1 red pepper, chopped into 3cm pieces
1 bulb of fennel, chopped into 3cm pieces
2 tablespoons rapeseed or olive oil
2 tablespoons freshly squeezed lime juice
2 teaspoons freshly ground black pepper
100g walnuts
100g mixed salad leaves
sea salt

FOR THE DRESSING
15g coriander, freshly chopped
1 teaspoon grated fresh ginger
2 garlic cloves, very finely chopped
½ teaspoon caster sugar
½ green chilli
1 tablespoon diced fresh mango (or
   rehydrate a slice of dried mango)
4 tablespoons rapeseed or olive oil
sea salt, to taste

1 Preheat your oven to 200°C/gas mark 6 and place a roasting tin on the middle shelf to heat up.

2 In a bowl, toss the chopped vegetables with the oil, lime juice, black pepper and a good pinch of sea salt, then tip into the preheated roasting tin and roast for 25–30 minutes or until the vegetables are tender and a little charred around the edges.

3 For the dressing, whisk together all the ingredients in a bowl, adding the oil gradually as you blend. If the consistency is a bit too thick, thin out with a little water. Season with salt, to taste.

4 Spread the walnuts out on a baking tray and roast in the still-hot oven for about 5 minutes until fragrant.

5 In a large bowl, toss together the roasted vegetables with the dressing and salad leaves. Divide between serving plates and scatter with the roasted walnuts.

CABBAGE AND COCONUT SALAD

SERVES 4

Nirmal's mother gave us this recipe. He grew up in the Chini Chini village on the Gujarati border, where this dish is popular, especially in family homes. It's a really simple dish and a beautiful way to eat cabbage. It's lovely on its own, or paired with rice or fish.

2 tablespoons coconut oil
1½ teaspoons mustard seeds
1½ teaspoons white urad dal, well rinsed
10 curry leaves (fresh are best if you can get them, but dried are fine)
4 green chillies, cut into diamond shape, sliced on the diagonal
2 teaspoons grated fresh ginger
½ large or 1 small cabbage, finely shredded
1 teaspoon sugar
½ teaspoon ground turmeric
freshly grated flesh from 1 coconut (see Note)
1 teaspoon freshly squeezed lemon juice
sea salt

1 Heat the oil in a non-stick frying pan, add the mustard seeds and wait for them to pop. Add the urad dal, curry leaves, green chillies and ginger and sauté over a medium heat for a few seconds, stirring continuously.

2 Add the shredded cabbage, sugar, turmeric and a good pinch of salt. Mix well and cook for 8–10 minutes, stirring once or twice. Add the coconut, reduce the heat and cook gently, stirring continuously, for 1–2 minutes. Sprinkle over the lemon juice and serve warm.

NOTE
To remove the flesh from a coconut, wrap the coconut in a clean tea towel. Set it in a metal bowl, still wrapped in the towel, and bash it a few times with a hammer or rolling pin until it cracks. Lift the coconut and the tea towel should strain out all the juice. Drink it or save for another use. Use the tip of a butter knife to prise the flesh from the coconut skin. Grate the flesh using a box grater or the grating attachment on your food processor.

BHUNA AUBERGINE
AND CRISPY KALE SALAD

Nirmal has a magical way with vegetables. Keen to introduce some lighter dishes onto the menu, he's created some amazing salads taking inspiration from English ingredients but adding Indian flavours. It's not often you see mango mixed with kale. Trust me, it works.

1 litre sunflower oil, for deep-frying
150g kale, destemmed, washed, dried and finely chopped
1 aubergine, chopped into 3cm pieces
1 tablespoon mango powder
1 tablespoon black salt (or 1 teaspoon sea salt)
½ teaspoon cumin seeds, toasted
100g Greek yogurt
4cm chunk of cucumber
250g cherry tomatoes, halved
100g pomegranate seeds
1 ripe mango, stoned, peeled and diced
sea salt, to taste

1 Heat the oil in a deep, heavy-based pan over a high heat. You want the temperature to reach 170°C. If you don't have a thermometer, you can test that the oil is hot enough by dropping in a grain of rice; if the rice floats to the top and has bubbles around it, your oil is ready for frying.

2 Fry the kale in the hot oil in small batches until it's crispy. Remove with a slotted spoon and drain on kitchen paper. Sprinkle each batch with a pinch of salt.

3 Keep the oil hot and fry the aubergine cubes in small batches until golden on all sides. Remove with a slotted spoon, drain on kitchen paper and sprinkle with half the mango powder and black or sea salt.

4 In a bowl, whisk the yogurt with the remaining mango powder and black salt, and half the toasted cumin seeds. Coarsely grate the cucumber, place in a sieve and squeeze out as much water as you can. Mix into the yogurt – and you have a cucumber raita.

5 To assemble the salad, spread a little cucumber raita over the base of your serving plates. Layer the cherry tomatoes on top, followed by the fried aubergine pieces and crispy kale. Finish with the pomegranate seeds, the mango and the remaining toasted cumin seeds. Serve straight away.

BANANA FLOWER AND SABUDANA CROQUETTES

SERVES 4

Nirmal loves banana flowers – they're one of his favourite ingredients. You can see the fresh flower in all its glory on page two of this book. It not only looks beautiful but it tastes wonderful, too. If you can't get hold of fresh banana flower, you can find it tinned (see Note), which works just as well. This is the first dish Nirmal ever made for me. I love it.

1 medium fresh banana flower (see Note)
1 teaspoon ground turmeric
1 large potato, boiled in its skin until fully tender
1 tablespoon grated fresh ginger
½ teaspoon ground cumin
2 tablespoons rapeseed or sunflower oil, plus extra for deep-frying
a pinch of finely chopped green chilli
2 tablespoons raisins, soaked in enough boiling water to cover for 15 minutes
3 tablespoons toasted coconut flakes
½ teaspoon caster sugar
2 teaspoons garam masala (shop-bought, or see page 161)
3 tablespoons roasted peanuts, lightly crushed
150g tapioca pearls, soaked overnight and drained
4 tablespoons cornflour
200g Panko breadcrumbs
sea salt

1 Prepare your banana blossom. To do this, chop the blossom and place in a bowl of water with ½ teaspoon ground turmeric – this stops the blossoms from turning black. Wash the blossom in this water. Bring a pan of salted water to the boil. Add the remaining ½ teaspoon ground turmeric to the water, along with the washed blossom.

2 Cook, covered, for 8–10 minutes or until the flower is soft but not mushy. Please monitor this, as some flowers might take less time, and some more. Drain in a colander and lightly mash the blossom with the back of your spatula.

3 Peel and mash the boiled potato with salt, to taste, until smooth. Set aside.

4 Mix the ginger and cumin with 2 teaspoons water to make a paste.

5 Set a frying pan over a medium heat. Add the 2 tablespoons oil. Once hot, stir in the chilli, followed by the ginger and cumin paste. Mix in the mashed banana blossom with a pinch of salt and cook for 6–8 minutes.

6 Drain the soaked raisins and add them to the pan, along with the mashed potato, toasted coconut and sugar. Cook for a minute and take off the heat.

7 Mix the garam masala, peanuts and drained tapioca into the banana mixture. Once the mixture is cool enough to handle, roll small portions between your palms into golf ball-sized croquette shapes. Transfer to the fridge for 15 minutes.

8 Whisk the cornflour with 4 tablespoons water to make a smooth, milk-like batter. Place the breadcrumbs on a flat plate.

9 Dip the croquettes in the batter and immediately roll in breadcrumbs, ensuring that all sides are thoroughly covered with the crumbs. Place on a clean plate.

10 At this stage, you can store the croquettes in the fridge for 3–4 days in an airtight container. Try to arrange them in a single layer to maintain the shapes.

11 Once you are ready to cook, heat enough oil for deep-frying in a deep, heavy-based pan over a medium heat. Deep-fry the croquettes (in batches, if necessary) for 5 minutes until the outer layer is deep golden and crisp.

12 These are delicious served with raita and salad.

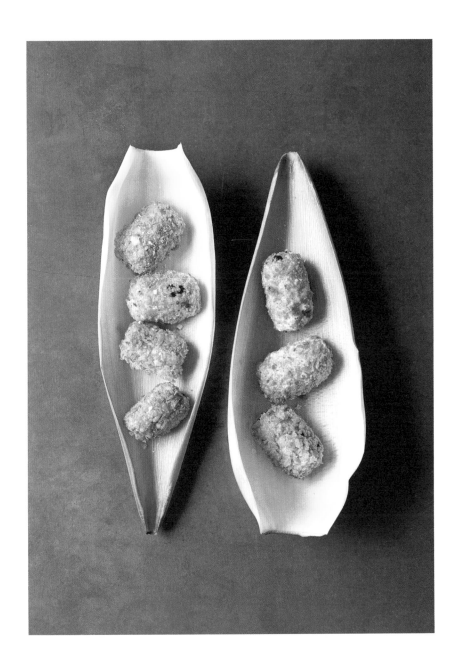

NOTE
You can use tinned banana blossom if you can't find fresh – it is available online
or in specialist Indian shops. You need 280g (drained weight).

SOUTH INDIAN CURD RICE

SERVES 4

Any time you have a bad tummy back home, this is what is served. The rice and yogurt have a soothing effect and the spices used are healing. Of course, you don't need to wait until you're suffering from a bad tummy to enjoy this! Eat it anytime – it's especially good with pickles on the side, or served as a cooling companion to a spicy dish.

400g cooked brown or white basmati rice
200g natural or Greek yogurt
2 tablespoons coconut oil or rapeseed oil
2 teaspoons yellow mustard seeds
1 teaspoon white urad dal, well rinsed
1 green chilli, finely chopped
6 curry leaves (fresh are best if you can get them, but dried are fine)
2 tablespoons freshly chopped coriander
sea salt

1 In a bowl, stir 1 tablespoon water into the rice and mash lightly using a potato masher. Mix in the yogurt and a pinch of salt, then cover and refrigerate for 1 hour.

2 Heat the oil in a small non-stick frying pan, add the mustard seeds and urad dal and sauté over a medium heat for 30 seconds. Add the green chilli and curry leaves and sauté for 30 seconds.

3 Fold the coriander through the chilled rice, then spoon over the oil and tempered spices. Serve straight away alongside a spicy meat dish, such as the Goan Pork on page 93.

ROASTED BHUTTA

SERVES 2

On the streets of India, people from the villages come to the market with portable barbecues when the sweetcorn comes into season because it's so fresh that you want to cook it then and there. The smell of the sweet butter fills the air and travels for miles, and the crack of the corn meeting the dancing flames is so hypnotic.

2 whole corn-on-the-cob
1½ tablespoons salted butter
a pinch of freshly ground black pepper

COCONUT CHILLI AND CORIANDER DRIZZLE
4 tablespoons grated fresh coconut
2 tablespoons freshly chopped coriander
a good pinch of chilli powder
a pinch of garlic salt
1½ tablespoons freshly squeezed lime juice
½ teaspoon rapeseed or olive oil

1 Remove the husks and silks from the corn, but keep the stem intact, which will help you handle the corn when you roast it.

2 Prepare a charcoal barbecue. Spread the butter over the corn and sprinkle with black pepper. Grill the corn over the barbecue for 10–15 minutes, rotating often to cook each side evenly. Alternatively, preheat the oven to 200°C/gas mark 6. Wrap the corn in foil and roast for 20–25 minutes.

3 While the corn cooks, mix the coconut with the coriander in a small bowl. In a separate bowl, whisk together the chilli powder, garlic salt, lime juice and oil.

4 Serve the roasted corn hot with the dressing drizzled all over the top. Finish with a generous sprinkle of the fresh coconut and coriander.

MASALA BHAAT

SERVES 6

Nirmal's wife wooed him with this dish. In India, cooking for someone is the ultimate expression of love. This one clearly won Nirmal over. It's a dish he loves serving and sharing with the customers at Gunpowder.

1 teaspoon coriander seeds
6 cloves
10 black peppercorns
2 teaspoons cumin seeds
2 tablespoons rapeseed or olive oil
2 onions, finely chopped
4 tablespoons grated fresh ginger
2 green chillies, finely chopped,
    or more/less to taste
½ teaspoon ground turmeric
a pinch of asafoetida
1 aubergine, cut into 1cm dice
300g basmati rice, soaked for 15 minutes
125g cluster beans (see Note) or French green
    beans, trimmed and cut into 4cm pieces
125g peas
6 tablespoons freshly chopped coriander
raita (see pages 176–183) or yogurt, to serve
sea salt

1 Heat a non-stick frying pan over a medium heat and toast the coriander seeds, cloves, black peppercorns and half the cumin seeds for a few seconds. Remove from the heat and allow to cool a little, transfer to a spice or coffee grinder or a pestle and mortar and grind to a powder. Set aside.

2 Heat the oil in a deep saucepan, add the remaining cumin seeds and sauté the onions for 5–10 minutes until soft and golden. Fold in the ginger and chillies and cook for a minute, then add the turmeric, asafoetida, aubergine and a good pinch of salt and fry for 10 minutes or until tender.

3 Stir in the rice, beans and peas. Add 600ml hot water and the ground spice mix you prepared earlier and mix well, then cover with a tightly fitting lid. Cook for 12–15 minutes or until all the water is absorbed by the rice.

4 Take off the heat and leave to steam for a further 5–10 minutes, then stir the chopped coriander through and serve with raita or just natural yogurt.

NOTE

In India, this would commonly be cooked with cluster beans. They look like smaller, flatter French green beans. If you can find them, they are great for this dish, but regular green beans work just as well.

BEEF PEPPER FRY

SERVES 4

For work, my dad had to go to South India a lot and this was a dish he came across in one of the canteens he'd stop by for food. For ten rupees you get the basic rice, lentils and salad. You then get to choose a meat or a fish to go alongside. I would sometimes travel with my dad on these trips and this was always one of my favourite canteen dishes.

2 rump or blade steaks (approx. 250g each), thinly sliced
2 tablespoons grated fresh ginger
1 green chilli, finely chopped
4 garlic cloves, finely chopped
2 teaspoons freshly ground black pepper
½ teaspoon ground coriander
½ teaspoon ground turmeric
a pinch of chilli powder
2 whole dried red chillies
50g coconut oil
1 teaspoon yellow mustard seeds
15 fresh curry leaves (dried will also work)
2 onions, thinly sliced
30g fresh coriander, chopped
30g coconut flakes, toasted
1 lime, cut into wedges

1 Place the sliced beef in a bowl with the ginger, green chilli, garlic, black pepper, ground coriander, turmeric and chilli powder and, using your fingers, massage the spices into the meat.

2 Set a frying pan with a lid over a high heat. When hot, add the beef and dried chillies (no oil is needed), cover and cook for 5–10 minutes or until the beef is cooked through. Remove the lid and continue cooking until all the moisture cooks down and coats the meat.

3 Meanwhile, in a separate pan, heat the coconut oil and add the mustard seeds and curry leaves. Let them sizzle for a few seconds, then add the onions and fry for about 5 minutes until golden brown. Fold in the cooked beef and chopped coriander and cook, stirring occasionally, for a further 5–10 minutes until the beef pepper fry turns a dark brown colour.

4 Serve immediately with the toasted coconut flakes and lime wedges on the side.

GRILLED AUBERGINE

with LAMB KEEMA and PINE NUT KACHUMBER

SERVES 4

Nirmal took part in a Cook for Syria fundraising event and this is the dish he created. It's a delicious and fragrant marriage of Indian and Persian spices.

FOR THE LAMB KEEMA
2 cinnamon sticks
3 green cardamom pods, bruised
5 cloves
2 tablespoons rapeseed or olive oil
2 onions, finely chopped
1 tablespoon grated fresh ginger
3 garlic cloves, finely chopped
1 green chilli chopped
2 tablespoons ground coriander
½ teaspoon garam masala (shop-bought, or see page 161)
½ teaspoon ground turmeric
½ teaspoon chilli powder
1 teaspoon ground cumin
2 large tomatoes, finely chopped
500g minced lamb
4 tablespoons freshly chopped coriander

FOR THE PINE NUT KACHUMBER
100g pine nuts
2 teaspoons rapeseed or olive oil
100g spring onions, finely chopped
1 green chilli, finely chopped
1 tomato, finely diced
2 tablespoon freshly chopped coriander
sea salt

FOR THE GRILLED AUBERGINE
2 large aubergines
1 tablespoon rapeseed or olive oil
2 teaspoons freshly ground black pepper

1 Set a large frying pan over a medium heat. Add the cinnamon, cardamom and cloves and dry-fry for 30 seconds. Add the oil and onion and sauté for 5 minutes, stirring occasionally, until golden brown.

2 Stir in the ginger, garlic and chilli. Cook for a minute, then add all the ground spices. Cook for a further minute.

3 Add the chopped tomatoes, stir and leave to simmer for 10–15 minutes or until the tomatoes have cooked down into a fairly thick paste.

4 Add the lamb mince and cook over a high heat for 5 minutes, stirring continuously. Reduce the heat to a gentle simmer and cook, covered, for about 10 minutes. Uncover and cook over a high heat for a further 5–10 minutes or until the mixture is fairly dry. Fold in the freshly chopped coriander. Set aside.

5 In a bowl, mix together all the ingredients for the pine nut kachumber. Season with salt, to taste.

6 Preheat your oven grill to high. Thinly slice the aubergine lengthways. Brush lightly with the oil and arrange on a grill pan. Cook under the grill for 4 minutes on each side, or until nicely golden. Season with the black pepper and a good pinch of salt.

7 Serve the beef mince on the top of the grilled aubergine, with the the pine nut kachumber sprinkled over the top.

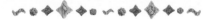

NAGALAND HOUSE BABY PORK RIBS

SERVES 4

My younger brother Avneet has a friend from Nagaland and his mother used to make this pork dish. We were lucky to get her recipe. You will love this dish. Of course, if you can't find naga or ghost chillies, you can use any other chilli, and add more or less to suit to your taste. The different layers of cooking in this recipe are what make it so special.

750ml apple juice
150g grated fresh ginger
2–3 naga chillies, split down the centre
8 whole star anise
1 slice fresh orange
75g soft light brown sugar
1kg baby back pork ribs
1 litre sunflower oil, for frying

FOR THE NAGA BBQ SAUCE
half the leftover stock from the braised ribs
75g (6 tablespoons) ketchup
100ml cider vinegar
50g honey
100g soft light brown sugar
25g tamarind paste
1 teaspoon crushed dried naga chillies,
   to taste
sea salt and freshly ground black pepper

FOR THE KACHUMBER SALAD
1 red onion
4 spring onions
1 tomato
½ cucumber, finely diced

TO SERVE
1 lime, for squeezing
a handful of fresh coriander, chopped

1 In a large saucepan with a lid, combine the apple juice, grated ginger, chillies, star anise, orange and brown sugar, stirring to mix well. Add the pork ribs and cover with about 1.5 litres water. Place over a high heat and bring to the boil, then simmer over a low heat for about 2½ hours, turning the ribs a few times, until tender.

2 Lift the ribs out of the stock, place on a chopping board and leave to cool. With a sharp knife, cut in between the ribs at two-rib intervals.

3 Strain half of the stock into a fresh pan (discard the remaining stock or reserve it for use in another recipe). Add the ketchup, cider vinegar, honey, sugar, tamarind and chillies and bring to the boil, then simmer over a low heat, stirring occasionally, until thickened, about 45 minutes. Season with salt and black pepper, to taste, then strain the sauce through a fine sieve into a bowl.

4 In a separate bowl, toss together all the ingredients for the kachumber salad.

5 Heat the oil in a deep, heavy-based pan over a high heat. Deep-fry the ribs in batches for 5 minutes until crispy and then dip into the sauce to glaze. Serve garnished with the kachumber salad, with a squeeze of lime and the chopped coriander, along with the remaining sauce for dipping.

TIPS

The cooked ribs can be refrigerated in their braising liquid overnight and reheated gently before grilling. The sauce can be stored in the fridge for up to 1 week.

TAWA KALIMIRCH CHICKEN

The marinade for the chicken here is very traditional. We would always have this at home – often with a whole chicken or with two wings and two breasts. The avocado dip gives it a modern twist – a very delicious one. It's a complete hit in the restaurant and is a quick dish to make at home.

2 boneless, skinless chicken breasts, sliced
1 tablespoon rapeseed or olive oil

FOR THE MARINADE
2 tablespoons rapeseed or olive oil
2 green chillies, or to taste
1 teaspoon tamarind paste
1 tablespoon grated fresh ginger
2 garlic cloves, very finely chopped
½ teaspoon freshly ground black pepper
½ cinnamon stick
2 cloves
sea salt, to taste

FOR THE AVOCADO DIP
1 ripe avocado
100g fresh coriander, chopped
2 tablespoons diced fresh mango
1 teaspoon grated fresh ginger
1 garlic clove, very finely chopped
½ teaspoon caster sugar
1 green chilli, finely chopped
sea salt, to taste

1 Place all the marinade ingredients in a blender and blend until smooth. Tip the marinade over the chicken slices and massage into the meat with your hands. Cover and place in the fridge for 2 hours or overnight.

2 Put all the dip ingredients in a blender and blend until smooth, adding 1 tablespoon water if necessary.

3 Heat the oil in a large frying pan and cook the chicken for 3–4 minutes on each side until cooked through. Serve warm with the avocado dip.

GINGER CHICKEN WINGS

This is Nirmal's favourite recipe. He is a huge fan of chicken wings. Given the chance, I think he'd eat them every day for breakfast, lunch and dinner. This is, of course, a gourmet version – and the best you'll taste.

1kg chicken wings
2 large thumb-sized pieces of fresh ginger, peeled
8 garlic cloves, peeled
6 green chillies
1 tablespoon whole black peppercorns
2 sprigs of curry leaves or 1 tablespoon crushed, dried curry leaves
2 tablespoons Madras curry powder (shop-bought, or use our All-in-one Curry Powder, page 157)
1 teaspoon ground turmeric
5 tablespoons freshly squeezed lemon juice
2 medium eggs, beaten
300g rice flour
½ teaspoon chilli powder
½ teaspoon freshly ground black pepper
1 litre sunflower oil, for deep-frying
sea salt

1 Prep the chicken wings by scoring them on both sides (this will help them to cook much faster). Arrange in a wide, shallow dish.

2 In a blender, food processor or pestle and mortar, blend or pound one of the pieces of ginger with the garlic, green chillies, whole black peppercorns, curry leaves, curry powder and turmeric with the lemon juice and a pinch of salt to make a coarse paste. Coat the chicken wings in the paste and marinate for 2–3 hours in the fridge.

3 Meanwhile, slice the other piece of ginger into thin matchsticks and set aside.

4 When you're ready to cook, pour the beaten eggs over the marinated chicken wings and turn to coat well.

5 Tip the rice flour into a dish or onto a plate and stir in the chilli powder and black pepper. Dredge the chicken wings through the flour, one by one, coating them thoroughly on all sides.

6 Heat the oil in a deep, heavy-based pan over a high heat to reach 170°C. Deep-fry the wings in small batches for 5–6 minutes until crispy and cooked. You can tell if they're cooked through by pricking the fattest part of the wing – the juices should run clear. If you're worried, finish them off on an oven preheated to 180°C/gas mark 4 for 10 minutes. After the chicken is fried, keep the oil hot and quickly drop in the ginger matchsticks. Cook for 1–2 minutes until crispy, then remove with a slotted spoon and drain on kitchen paper.

7 Serve the wings with your choice of dip (see pages 176–183), garnished with the crispy ginger and an extra sprinkling of salt.

PICKLED SCALLOPS

with WILD GARLIC AND CUMIN CAULIFLOWER

SERVES 2–4

Nirmal loves seafood, with scallops being a particular favourite. He's created a wonderful sauce to go with them here made with the springtime flush of wild garlic, but you can swap it out for chives when wild garlic is out of season.

FOR THE SCALLOPS
8 shelled king scallops, rinsed and dried
1 teaspoon naga chilli pickle
  (or any hot chilli sauce)
sea salt

FOR THE WILD GARLIC CHUTNEY
100g wild garlic (or use chives when
  wild garlic is not in season)
30g fresh coriander, chopped
½ teaspoon cumin seeds
2 garlic cloves
1 green chilli, or to taste
1 teaspoon freshly squeezed lime juice
1 tablespoon rapeseed or olive oil

FOR THE CUMIN CAULIFLOWER
½ cauliflower (approx. 100g),
  broken into florets
2 tablespoons rapeseed or olive oil
1 teaspoon cumin seeds
1 teaspoon grated fresh ginger
½ green chilli, chopped
¼ teaspoon ground turmeric
1 tablespoon freshly squeezed lime juice

1 Place the scallops in a shallow dish with the naga chilli pickle and a pinch of salt. Cover and leave to marinate in the fridge for 1 hour.

2 Place all the chutney ingredients in a blender and blend until smooth. Season with salt to taste and loosen with 1–2 tablespoons water, if necessary.

3 Blanch the cauliflower in a pan of boiling water for 2 minutes, then drain and refresh under cold water to prevent further cooking.

4 Heat the oil in a frying pan over a high heat and, once hot, add the cumin seeds, ginger, chilli and turmeric and stir together. Add the cauliflower and toss well to coat in the spices. Season with salt, to taste, and the lime juice and set aside.

5 Heat a non-stick frying pan over a high heat until just smoking and sear the scallops for 1 minute on each side until you see a golden brown crust.

6 Spread a little wild garlic chutney on each serving plate, top with the seared scallops and add a spoonful of the cumin cauliflower on the side.

LOBSTER BALCHAO

SERVES 2

In India, if you want to escape for the holidays, Goa is the place to go. This dish is very much inspired by the cuisine of Goa and of memories of family holidays there.

2 raw lobster tails
1 tablespoon freshly squeezed lemon juice
½ teaspoon ground turmeric
4 dried red chillies
½ teaspoon black peppercorns
1 cinnamon stick
4 cloves
50ml malt vinegar
1 teaspoon grated fresh ginger
2 tablespoons rapeseed or olive oil
1 onion, finely chopped
2 garlic cloves, very finely chopped
2 tomatoes, finely chopped
1 teaspoon jaggery
sea salt

1 To prepare the lobster tails, use a sharp knife or kitchen scissors to cut the tail lengthways down from the centre and remove any veins. Rinse well and pat dry.

2 Place the tails in a shallow dish with the lemon juice and turmeric. Season with salt and marinate in the fridge until you are ready to use.

3 In a spice or coffee grinder or pestle and mortar, finely grind the chillies, black peppercorns, cinnamon stick and cloves to a powder. Mix with the malt vinegar, ginger and a pinch of salt to make a paste.

4 Place a wide, heavy-based pan over a high heat, then reduce the heat to medium and cook the onion for 5 minutes until soft and golden. Add the spice paste and cook for a minute until fragrant, then add the lobster and simmer, stirring continuously, for 5 minutes. Add the tomatoes and cook for 6–8 minutes until they break down and form a sauce, then stir through the jaggery and salt to balance the flavours. Check the lobster meat to ensure it's cooked through – to do this, insert a small knife into the centre of the fattest part and pry it open. It should be white all the way through. Cook for a little longer if needed.

5 Serve warm. This is delicious with rice and a salad.

MASALA FISH CAKES

In Kolkata, we eat so much seafood, even to begin the day. In fact, my mum makes these for breakfast, and typically we'd eat them sandwiched between white bread – our take on a fish finger sandwich!

400g skinless whiting, cod or haddock, rinsed and dried
¼ teaspoon ground turmeric
a pinch of sea salt
600g floury potatoes, peeled and boiled
1 teaspoon grated fresh ginger
1 green chilli, finely chopped
½ teaspoon cumin seeds, toasted and ground
2 tablespoons finely chopped coriander
½ teaspoon freshly ground black pepper
½ teaspoon garam masala (shop-bought, or see page 161)
2 medium eggs
200g panko breadcrumbs
sunflower or rapeseed oil, for shallow frying
your choice of dip (see pages 176–183), to serve

1 Place the fish in a wide, deep pan with a lid and sprinkle over the turmeric and salt. Pour in enough water to fully submerge, then cover and simmer over a medium heat for 10 minutes. Strain and, once cooled, flake the fish onto a plate.

2 Grate the cooked potatoes into a bowl. Add the fish, ginger, chilli, cumin, coriander, black pepper and garam masala and mix together well. Using your hands, shape the mixture into eight patties.

3 Whisk the eggs together in a shallow dish and place the panko breadcrumbs in a separate shallow dish.

4 Dip each fish cake in the beaten egg and then in the panko breadcrumbs, then repeat the process so that they are thoroughly coated. Refrigerate for 30 minutes (or pop in the freezer for 15 minutes).

5 Heat a shallow pool of oil in a non-stick frying pan and, when hot, fry the fish cakes for about 4 minutes on each side, until golden and crisp. Add more oil to the pan, if necessary. Serve warm with your chosen dip.

ETTI MASALA
(SOUTH INDIAN-STYLE PRAWNS)

SERVES 2–4

Nirmal and I cemented our friendship over a few drinks – quite a few drinks, actually – and this is just the dish you need for such a drinking session. It's especially good with a cold glass of beer, but you could also make it as a generous garnish for the Malabar Prawn Pulao (see page 123).

juice of 1 lime
1 tablespoon ground turmeric
1 tablespoon ground coriander
1 teaspoon freshly ground black pepper
12 raw jumbo king prawns, in their shells
1 small onion, finely chopped
5 garlic cloves, very finely chopped
10 curry leaves (fresh are best if you can get them, but dried are fine), plus 6 extra leaves to garnish
1½ tablespoons coconut oil
1½ tablespoons rapeseed oil
1 teaspoon green peppercorns, to garnish
sea salt

1 In a bowl, mix together the lime juice, turmeric, ground coriander, black pepper and a pinch of salt. Add the prawns and turn to coat thoroughly, then cover and set aside to marinate for 15 minutes.

2 Heat the coconut oil in a non-stick frying pan over a high heat. Once melted, cook the onion with a pinch of salt for about 5 minutes until soft and lightly caramelised. Add the garlic and 10 of the curry leaves and cook for 2 minutes until golden.

3 Add the marinated prawns and gently fry for 5 minutes until the mix is a little dry and the prawns get a nice colour on them. Remove the prawn from the pan and keep warm. Quickly heat the rapeseed oil in the hot pan and fry the remaining curry leaves until crispy.

4 Serve the prawns hot, sprinkled with the green peppercorns and fried curry leaves.

MUSSELS RASSA

You could say that this recipe is a fisherman's cheat, as it's rather simple and quick. The key is in using really fresh mussels so all their beautiful juices seep into the sauce. This is why we call it a fisherman's cheat – because the fisherman does most of the work!

4 tablespoons coconut oil
1 teaspoon yellow mustard seeds
8 garlic cloves, finely sliced
1 thumb-sized piece of fresh ginger, peeled and chopped into matchsticks
4 green chillies, halved lengthways
10 curry leaves (fresh are best if you can get them, but dried are fine)
1 small onion or 2 shallots, thinly sliced
1 teaspoon ground turmeric
1 teaspoon Madras curry powder (shop-bought, or use our All-in-one Curry Powder, page 163)
½ teaspoon chilli powder
200ml fish stock
800g mussels in their shells, rinsed, scrubbed and drained (discard any that don't close in response to a tap)
100ml coconut cream
a pinch of sugar
sea salt

TO SERVE
2 tablespoons finely chopped coriander
½ lime
plain rice (optional)

1 Heat the oil in a large flameproof casserole dish with a lid, add the mustard seeds and wait for them to pop, then add the garlic, ginger, green chillies and curry leaves and cook, stirring, for a minute.

2 Add the onion or shallots and gently cook for 5 minutes, then stir through the turmeric, curry and chilli powders. Pour in the fish stock and cook over a medium–high heat, stirring occasionally, until slightly reduced – about 15 minutes.

3 Add the cleaned mussels and coconut cream, stir and cover with the lid. Cook for 3–4 minutes until all the mussels have opened (discard any that remain closed), then season with the sugar (to balance the spices and heat) and salt, to taste.

4 Scatter with the chopped coriander and serve the mussels hot on with a squeeze of lime, either on their own or with plain rice.

BIG
PLATES

BIG PLATES

Indian families are always massive and the best way to get everyone together is over a large home-cooked meal. We show our love and affection through food, and dining together is when we connect the most. Typically, these gatherings of cousins, uncles, aunties, mothers, fathers, their children and dear friends is as much about exchanging information – all the banter, gossip, opinions and news – as it is about sharing age-old recipes that have been handed down over many years, evolving with each new generation.

The following recipes are the ones we've harvested, shared and grown. They're a collection of memories, delicious ones at that, and ones we hope you'll savour with those you cherish, too.

You don't need a celebration to make these dishes – the love and art of preparing them is a special occasion itself. The joy of these recipes is that they make larger portions that can be served communally. If you're lucky, you'll end up with leftovers, so you can keep feasting as the week rolls on.

ACHARI PARTRIDGE

with PICKLED YOGURT DIP and ROASTED PINEAPPLE SALAD

SERVES 4

This is a famous recipe in the south west of India, where game dishes are very popular. The first marinade is almost like a pickle – it gives the meat so much flavour and renders it so tender before it hits the grill.

2 red partridge legs, cut in
   half lengthways

FOR THE FIRST MARINADE
4 tablespoons freshly squeezed
   lemon juice
2 teaspoons grated fresh ginger
2 garlic cloves, very finely chopped
½ teaspoon chilli powder
1 teaspoon sea salt

FOR THE SECOND MARINADE
200g Greek yogurt
4 tablespoons lime pickle
1 tablespoon grated fresh ginger
1 green chilli, finely chopped
1 teaspoon dried fenugreek leaves
1 teaspoon nigella seeds
2 tablespoons mustard or
   rapeseed oil
½ teaspoon chilli powder, or to taste
sea salt, to taste

FOR THE ROASTED PINEAPPLE SALAD
1 pineapple, peeled, cored and
   cut into 2cm-thick slices
2 tablespoons honey
2 teaspoons chaat masala
1 teaspoon freshly ground
   black pepper
1 teaspoon caster sugar
4 spring onions, finely chopped
1 green chilli, finely chopped

FOR THE PICKLED YOGURT DIP
250g Greek yogurt
1 teaspoon naga chilli pickle,
   or to taste
½ teaspoon caster sugar

1 In a large bowl, mix together all the ingredients for the first marinade. Toss the partridge in the mixture until thoroughly coated, then cover and set aside to marinate for 30 minutes.

2 In a separate bowl, mix together the ingredients for the second marinade, then pour over the marinating partridge and stir to coat. Cover and refrigerate for 3 hours, or overnight.

3 Preheat your oven grill to high. In a bowl, mix the pineapple slices with the honey, chaat masala, black pepper and sugar and then set aside to marinate for 15 minutes. Arrange the pineapple slices on a baking tray in a single layer. Grill for 5–10 minutes on each side or until each side is nicely coloured. Set aside to cool, then chop into small dice and mix with the spring onion and green chilli. Refrigerate until ready to eat.

4 In a small bowl, mix together all the ingredients for the pickled yogurt dip.

5 When you're ready to cook, preheat your grill to high. Arrange the partridge in a shallow ovenproof dish and grill for 10 minutes on each side until cooked through. Test by piercing the fattest part of the meat with a skewer or sharp knife. The juices should be clear. If not, cook for a little longer.

6 Serve hot with the pickled yogurt dip and roasted pineapple salad on the side.

GHEE ROAST PEPPER QUAIL
with GUNPOWDER DOSA

SERVES 4

Nirmal is a master when it comes to preparing game dishes. These are all recipes inspired by his home village, where game is eaten far more often than chicken. The dosa can be paired with lots of other recipes in the book, such as the Market-style Scrambled Eggs (see page 20). This recipe requires overnight marinating and fermenting. *Pictured on pages 84–85.*

4 whole quails, butterflied (you can ask your butcher to do this)
2 tablespoons ghee
12 fresh curry leaves
2 onions, finely chopped
2 garlic cloves, finely chopped
2 teaspoons freshly ground black pepper

FOR THE MARINADE
2 tablespoons freshly squeezed lemon juice
2 teaspoons grated fresh ginger
2 garlic cloves, very finely chopped
1 green chilli, finely chopped
2 teaspoons garam masala (shop-bought, or see page 161)
1 teaspoon freshly ground black pepper
½ teaspoon ground turmeric
½ teaspoon red chilli powder, to taste
1 drop of cinnamon essential oil or 1 teaspoon ground cinnamon
sea salt, to taste

FOR THE DOSA
100g urad dal flour (see Tip)
150g rice flour
1 teaspoon sea salt
500ml filtered or mineral water
2–3 tablespoons rapeseed or olive oil
1 tablespoon Gunpowder Spice Mix (see page 158)

1 In a large bowl, mix together all the ingredients for the marinade. Add the quails and toss to coat well, then marinate for 4 hours or overnight in the fridge.

2 To make the dosa, mix together the flours and salt in a bowl and, little by little, add the filtered or mineral water to make a thick batter. Keep mixing as you add the water and stop when the batter is the consistency of double cream.

3 Cover the batter and set aside in a warm place to ferment for 8 hours or overnight. It should be quite bubbly and airy once it's fermented. However, it might also have thickened, so before cooking you may need to add a little more water to return it to the consistency of double cream.

4 Place a large frying pan over a high heat and add enough oil to gloss the surface of the pan. Add 2–3 tablespoons of dosa batter, swirl around the base to coat evenly and cook both sides until golden brown. Sprinkle a pinch of gunpowder spice over the cooked dosa and remove from the pan. Continue until you've

used up all the batter (you should get about eight dosa). Set aside.

5 Place the quail and all of the marinade in a large, lidded flameproof casserole dish over a medium heat. Pop the lid on snugly, reduce the heat and cook until the quail is tender, about 30–35 minutes. If there is liquid left, cook on a slightly higher heat to evaporate it. Once cooked, set aside, still covered, for 30 minutes to rest.

6 Place a large frying pan over a medium heat. When hot, add the ghee and fry the curry leaves until crisp, then remove and set aside. Add the onion and garlic to the pan and cook, stirring, for 5 minutes until soft and a little golden. Add the quails along with any marinade and sprinkle over the black pepper. Fry for 5–10 minutes until all the pepper, quail, ghee and cinnamon aromas are released, then take off the heat.

7 Garnish with the crispy curry leaves and serve hot with the dosa.

TIP

If you have a spice or coffee grinder, you can make your own urad dal flour by simply grinding urad dal lentils to a fine powder.

PHEASANT BHUJING PULAO

SERVES 2–4

Nirmal's mother makes this wonderful dish – it's a family favourite. It's incredibly comforting and unusual in that it uses rice flakes, making it rather like a savoury porridge. But you can easily make it more biryani-like by using cooked white or brown basmati rice instead.

1 whole pheasant, skinned and cut into 8 pieces
6 baby potatoes, peeled and sliced into 1cm-thick rounds
3 tablespoons rapeseed or olive oil
6 cloves
1 cinnamon stick
6 black peppercorns
4 green cardamom pods
2 onions, finely chopped
1 teaspoon ground turmeric
a pinch of chilli powder
1 teaspoon ground cumin
1 teaspoon ground coriander
1 teaspoon garam masala (shop-bought, or see page 161)
250g medium-sized rice flakes
sea salt, to taste

FOR THE MARINADE
4 tablespoons Greek yogurt
50g fresh coriander, chopped
10 mint leaves
1 green chilli
3 garlic cloves, very finely chopped
1 tablespoon grated fresh ginger

TO SERVE
chopped fresh coriander
freshly squeezed lime juice
your choice of Raita (see pages 176–183)

1 For a superior, smoky flavour, prepare a charcoal barbecue. If you don't have one, preheat your oven grill to high.

2 Blitz the marinade ingredients together in a food processor or pestle and mortar to make a thick paste. Rub half the paste into the pheasant pieces and baby potatoes and leave to marinate for 30 minutes. Reserve the rest.

3 On the barbecue or grill, grill the marinated pheasant pieces for about 10 minutes, turning once or twice. Parboil the sliced potatoes in a pan with just enough salted water to cover them for about 10 minutes, until just tender.

4 Meanwhile, set a large pan with a lid over a medium heat. Add the oil and, once hot, add the cloves, cinnamon, peppercorns and cardamom pods, followed by the onions. Gently fry until golden – about 10 minutes.

5 Fold through the remaining spices and the rest of the green paste. Add a pinch of salt and 250ml water. Cover and cook for 10 minutes.

6 Fold the grilled pheasant and potatoes through the sauce and cook for 10 minutes.

7 Add the rice and check that the quantity of sauce is just enough to soak the rice flakes – if not, top up with enough water to cover by 2cm. Simmer for just long enough to soften the rice flakes, and take off the heat. Stir in the fresh coriander and a squeeze lime, to taste. Serve with your choice of Raita.

TIP

Rice flakes (*poha*) go dry after a while, so serve immediately. If you can't find rice flakes, you can swap them out with cooked basmati rice.

MALVANI SUKKA CHICKEN

Malvan is a coastal area in Konkan, which has its own distinct way of cooking food. The region's cuisine is famous for using coconut liberally. Dried red chillies and cardamom are also dominant features in local dishes. The sauce for this gorgeous chicken is so beautiful – it's lovely served with rice or dosas (see page 86) to help mop it all up.

8 chicken drumsticks
4 whole dried kashmiri chillies
2 teaspoons coriander seeds
4 cloves
½ teaspoon black peppercorns
½ teaspoon cumin seeds
seeds from 5 green cardamom pods
seeds from 2 black cardamom pods
1 tablespoon desiccated coconut
1 teaspoon poppy seeds
2 teaspoons fennel seeds
2 star anise
½ cinnamon stick
4 tablespoons rapeseed or coconut oil
2 large onions, finely chopped
a handful of freshly chopped coriander,
   to garnish
sea salt

1 Score the chicken drumsticks by piercing them all over with the tip of a sharp knife; this will help them cook faster and absorb all the flavours from the sauce.

2 Place a frying pan over a medium heat and dry-roast the chillies for a minute. Set aside.

3 In the same pan, dry-roast the coriander seeds, cloves, black peppercorns, cumin seeds, green and black cardamom seeds, desiccated coconut, poppy seeds, fennel seeds, star anise and cinnamon for 1–2 minutes until all their aromas are released. Set aside to cool.

4 Combine the spices in a pestle and mortar or spice grinder and grind to a powder. For extra heat, grind the dry-roasted chillies, too, or add them to the dish whole for a milder heat. Transfer the ground spices to a bowl and whisk in 150ml warm water to create a smooth paste. Set aside.

5 Heat the oil in a sauté pan over a medium heat. Add the onions and a pinch of salt and cook for 4 minutes. Stir in the prepared spice paste (and the whole chillies if you didn't grind them) and cook for 15 seconds.

6 Add the chicken drumsticks with 120ml water and stir well to incorporate. Cook for 30 minutes, stirring occasionally. Once you see oil starting to release from the sides of the sauce, turn off the heat.

7 Garnish with chopped coriander and serve the chicken hot with the sauce spooned over the top.

ORGANIC TANDOORI CHICKEN

SERVES 4

Every Indian boy worth his salt likes a good tandoori chicken. Of course, every family has their own take on the iconic dish, but we have to say ours is pretty special. The fenugreek and mango powder give it that magic touch.

1.4 kg whole organic chicken or 4 chicken legs
2 garlic cloves, finely chopped
1 tablespoon grated fresh ginger
1 green chilli, finely chopped
2 tablespoons freshly squeezed lime juice
1 tablespoon mustard or rapeseed oil
2 tablespoons Greek yogurt
2 tablespoons finely chopped coriander
1 tablespoon smoked paprika
½ tablespoon mango powder
½ tablespoon garam masala (shop-bought, or see page 161)
½ tablespoon dried fenugreek leaves
1 tablespoon ground coriander
½ tablespoon ground cumin
3 tablespoons Kashmiri chilli oil (see Tip)

1 If you're using a whole chicken, remove the giblets (if it has them). Using a large, sharp knife, cut down through the breastbone of the chicken, prise the bird open and cut down through the backbone so that the chicken is in two identical halves – each with a breast, leg and wing. Alternatively, you can just use four chicken legs.

2 Pull the skin off the chicken and, using a knife again, score the fatter parts of the chicken legs and breast as this will help them cook faster and absorb all the flavours from the marinade.

3 In a bowl, mix together the garlic, ginger and chilli with the lime juice and mustard or rapeseed oil. Use your hands to rub this all over the chicken, then set aside for 10 minutes.

4 In a separate bowl, mix together all the remaining ingredients to form a paste, then rub this all over the chicken, too. Cover and marinate for 30 minutes (or you can leave it in the fridge overnight).

5 Prepare a charcoal barbecue or preheat your oven to 220°C/gas mark 7. If using a barbecue, thread the marinated chicken onto skewers and turn regularly to cook all sides evenly. This should take about 15–20 minutes. Alternatively, arrange the chicken on a grill pan and cook in the oven for about 40 minutes or until nicely charred all over and cooked all the way through. You can test by piercing the fattest part of the chicken and seeing if the juices run clear – if not, cook a little longer. Rest for 20 minutes before serving.

6 Serve with Bhurani raita (see page 176) and salad.

TIP

To make your own Kashmiri chilli oil, simply infuse two broken Kashmiri chillies in a bottle with 250ml olive or rapeseed oil for two weeks. For a faster infusion, heat the oil, add the chillies and gently warm for 15 minutes, then infuse for a further 15 minutes and strain.

DUM-PUKTH CHICKEN

SERVES 4

Dum is a very special way of cooking meat or fish from northern India. The *dum* refers to sealing the pot with a simple flour, salt and water-based dough. The seal locks in the moisture and lets the meat or fish steam in its own juices. This dish has a large amount of fenugreek leaves – you can use dried or fresh. They're incredibly good for you, especially for your digestion. My wife and I eat this dish a lot at home.

8 chicken thighs
1 tablespoon grated fresh ginger
8 garlic cloves, finely chopped
1–2 green chillies, finely chopped
6 tablespoons freshly chopped coriander, plus extra to garnish
2 tablespoons ghee
1 onion, finely chopped
2 tablespoons Greek yogurt
2 bay leaves
8 tablespoons fenugreek leaves
1 teaspoon ground cumin
1 teaspoon ground coriander
½ teaspoon ground mace
ground seeds from 16 green cardamom pods
fresh coriander, to garnish
sea salt

FOR THE DOUGH (FOR SEALING THE DISH)
250g plain flour
2 tablespoons olive or rapeseed oil

1 Using a sharp knife, score each chicken thigh about 1cm deep at 2–3cm intervals, as this will help the meat absorb all the flavours from the dish.

2 In a bowl, mix together the ginger, garlic, green chilli and half the fresh coriander to make a paste.

3 Place a sauté pan over a medium heat, add half the ghee and, once melted, cook the onion with a pinch of salt until it's nicely golden. Transfer to a blender and blend to make a fine paste, then stir into the ginger paste and whisk in the yogurt. Slather this marinade over the chicken, cover and marinate in the fridge for 6 hours or overnight.

4 Remove the chicken from the fridge and bring up to room temperature before using.

5 For the dough, mix together the flour, 100ml water and the oil in a bowl until the mixture resembles uncooked pastry. Add a little more flour or water if necessary.

6 Place a flameproof casserole dish with a lid over a medium heat. Add the remaining ghee, together with the bay leaves and marinated chicken and cook until it starts to brown a little all over.

7 Add the fenugreek leaves with the cumin and ground coriander and stir well. The heap of fenugreek will make it look a little dry, but once you cover the pot, the steam inside will keep everything tender and moist.

8 Cover the dish with the lid and seal using the dough. Cook over a low heat for 35 minutes until the chicken is cooked through and the flavours are all released.

9 Sprinkle the chicken with the ground mace and cardamom and serve hot garnished with chopped coriander. This is delicious with salad and rice.

GOAN PORK

In Goa, they eat pork because the region is predominantly Christian. Of course, in Muslim regions of India, pork does not feature. At Gunpowder, Nirmal favours pork from Gloucestershire Old Spots. The use of vinegar in this dish is very traditional. Dishes like 'vin'-daloo reference the use of vinegar, which really balance the flavours.

500g boneless pork, diced
4 tablespoons rapeseed or olive oil
2 onions, finely chopped
1 tablespoon grated fresh ginger
3 garlic cloves, very finely chopped
2 whole dried red chillies
4 tablespoons red wine vinegar
cooked red Goan rice, to serve (available online, in Indian stores and in larger supermarkets)
sea salt

FOR THE MARINADE
1 tablespoon coriander seeds
1 teaspoon cumin seeds
½ teaspoon black peppercorns
1 cinnamon stick
3 cloves
1 teaspoon grated fresh ginger
2 garlic cloves, peeled
1 teaspoon ground turmeric
1 teaspoon brown sugar
1 teaspoon yellow mustard seeds
½ teaspoon fenugreek seeds

1 Begin with the marinade. Place a frying pan over a medium heat and toast all the whole spices for the marinade for 1–2 minutes or until fragrant. Leave to cool a little, then transfer them to a pestle and mortar or spice grinder. Grind them to a fine powder, then mix with the other marinade ingredients. Rub the mixture into the pork all over, cover and marinate in the fridge for 4 hours, or overnight.

2 When you're ready to cook, heat the oil in a sauté pan with a lid over a medium heat. Once hot, stir in the onions with a pinch of salt and gently fry for about 5 minutes until golden. Add the ginger and garlic and cook for 30 seconds, then add the marinated pork, along with the dried chillies and vinegar.

3 Fry the pork for 10 minutes until a little golden on each side, then add 250ml water and bring to the boil. Reduce the heat, cover with the lid and cook for 45 minutes until the meat is tender.

4 Serve with red Goan rice.

WILD RABBIT PULAO

We call this Aunty Sulu's pulao. It comes from Nirmal's mother. She made this for me after Nirmal and his wife had their first child. I brought a gift to the house and in exchange she asked me what I'd like her to cook for me. I'd tried her famous rabbit pulao before, so this was the dish I requested.

1 whole wild rabbit (approx. 800g), prepared and cut into 5–6 pieces
300g basmati rice
100g dried cranberries or sour cherries
3 tablespoons olive or rapeseed oil
2 tablespoons ghee
2 onions, thinly sliced
250ml vegetable stock
6 green cardamom pods
8 cloves
1 cinnamon stick
1 bay leaf
12 strands of saffron, soaked in 2 tablespoons warm water for 10 minutes to release the colour and aroma
2 tablespoons freshly squeezed lemon juice
30g freshly chopped mint leaves, to garnish
30g freshly chopped coriander, to garnish
sea salt

FOR THE MARINADE
2 tablespoons grated fresh ginger
4 garlic cloves, very finely chopped
4 tablespoons natural yogurt
1 green chilli, finely chopped
a pinch of chilli powder
1 tablespoon ground turmeric
5 tablespoons finely chopped mint leaves
5 tablespoons freshly chopped coriander
2 tablespoons garam masala (shop-bought, or see page 161)

1 Check over the rabbit and remove any shot remnants you might find (they'll be little lead dots the size of a coriander seed or smaller).

2 In a large bowl, mix together all the marinade ingredients and then use your hands to rub the mixture into the meat. Cover and marinate in the fridge for 6 hours, or overnight. Bring up to room temperature before using.

3 Place the rice in a dish, cover with water and soak for 30 minutes. Place the cranberries or cherries in a separate dish and cover with water. Add a pinch of salt.

4 Heat 2 tablespoons of the oil and the ghee in a sauté pan with a lid over a medium heat. Stir in the onion with a large pinch of salt, as this will help draw the moisture from the onion and speed up the cooking. Sauté for 5 minutes until dark brown.

5 Add the rabbit with all the marinade and cook until nicely coloured all over. Pour in the vegetable stock and stir well, then cover with the lid. Reduce the heat and simmer gently for 1 hour.

6 In the meantime, pour 600ml water into a large saucepan. Add the cardamom, cloves, cinnamon and bay and bring to the boil over a medium heat. Reduce the heat, cover with a lid and simmer for 15 minutes or so until all the flavours from the whole spices infuse the water. Add the remaining oil and ½ teaspoon salt, then drain your soaking rice and add to the boiling water. Cook for 12 minutes or until all the water has been absorbed. Take off the heat but keep the lid on to let it steam through for a further 5 minutes.

7 Check that the rabbit is tender, then take off the heat and mix with the rice. Strain the cranberries or cherries and stir through the dish together with the saffron, soaking water and all. Season with salt, to taste, and finish with the lemon juice and freshly chopped mint and coriander.

KOSBADI RABBIT MASALA

SERVES 2–4

This is another famous rabbit dish from Nirmal's mother, nicknamed Aunty Sulu. The recipe gets its name from Kosbad, which is a village in the Palghar district of Maharashtra.

2 tablespoons rapeseed
   or coconut oil
4 cloves
½ cinnamon stick
1 onion, finely chopped
¼ teaspoon ground turmeric
1 tomato, finely chopped
4 rabbit legs, each leg cut into
   3 pieces (see Tip), rinsed and dried
sea salt

FOR THE SPICE PASTE
3–4 dried Kashmiri chillies
2 teaspoons coriander seeds
1 teaspoon cumin seeds
1 teaspoon black peppercorns
4 garlic cloves, very finely chopped
1 tablespoon, grated fresh ginger
2 tablespoons natural yogurt

TO GARNISH AND TO SERVE
100ml rapeseed or sunflower oil
1 small onion or shallot, thinly sliced
1 thumb-sized piece of fresh ginger,
   peeled and julienned
a handful of mint leaves,
   finely chopped
lemon wedges

1 Place a frying pan over a high heat. Add the chillies and cook for 30 seconds. Reduce the heat to medium, add the coriander seeds, cumin seeds and peppercorns and toast for 2 minutes or until fragrant, then leave to cool a little. Transfer to a spice grinder or pestle and mortar and grind to a fine powder. Place in a bowl with the garlic, ginger and yogurt and mix together to make a paste.

2 Heat the oil in a flameproof casserole dish with a lid over a high heat. Once hot, stir in the cloves and cinnamon and fry until aromatic, then fold in the onion and cook for 5 minutes until golden.

3 Add the turmeric and tomato and cook for 5–10 minutes until the tomato has broken down and darkened a little.

4 Add the rabbit and fry for 3–4 minutes, then add 150ml water and a pinch of salt. Stir well to incorporate, then cover with the lid and cook for a further 5–6 minutes.

5 Remove the lid, stir in the spice paste and cook for a few more minutes until the sauce has been absorbed and the rabbit is tender but cooked through – it should be starting to pull away from the bone. Season with a little more salt, to taste.

6 For the garnishes, heat the oil in a small, deep saucepan until bubbling hot, then add the onion or shallot and cook until golden. Remove with a slotted spoon and drain on kitchen paper. Add the ginger to the hot oil and fry until golden, then drain on kitchen paper and dust with a little salt.

7 Serve the rabbit sprinkled with the fried onion, crispy ginger and fresh mint leaves, and with lemon wedges on the side.

TIP

You can easily cut through the bones of the rabbit with a sharp cook's knife or bread knife, or you can ask you butcher to do this for you. You could also swap the four legs used here for a whole rabbit, cut into 5–6 pieces.

KOLHAPURI LAMB SHANKS

SERVES 4

If you have friends coming over for dinner, this is a wonderful dish to make. It comes from Nirmal's village. It's a slow-cooking dish, so it takes a while, but once you put it in the pot, you don't have to do anything – just let it simmer away until the meat falls apart. If you're lucky enough to have leftovers the next day, shred the meat, sandwich it between two slices of white bread, add a little mustard inside and fry the sandwich in butter – or brush the outside with mayo and grill it (this sounds odd, but it creates the most wonderful crust). Leftovers are also wonderful fried with rice.

3 tablespoons coconut or
   rapeseed oil
2 onions, finely chopped
1 teaspoon ground turmeric
½ teaspoon asafoetida
1 tablespoon grated fresh ginger
3 garlic cloves, finely chopped
2 tomatoes, finely diced
4 lamb shanks (approx. 250g each),
   excess fat trimmed
3 tablespoons deggi mirch
   spice blend (see Note)
2 teaspoons yellow chilli powder
   (see Note)
1 tablespoon garam masala (shop-
   bought, or see page 161)
1 litre vegetable or lamb stock
100g freshly grated coconut
   (see Note on page 51)
2 teaspoons sesame seeds
2 teaspoons poppy seeds
1 thumb-sized piece of fresh ginger,
   peeled and julienned, to serve
freshly chopped coriander, to serve
sea salt

1 Heat the oil in a flameproof casserole dish with a lid over a medium heat and cook the onions for 5 minutes until translucent. Stir in the turmeric, asafoedita, ginger, garlic and tomatoes and sizzle, stirring often, for 10 minutes or until the tomatoes have broken down into a thick sauce.

2 Add the lamb shanks and sauté for 5 minutes and until coated all over in the thickened sauce. Stir in the deggi mirch, yellow chilli powder, garam masala and a pinch of salt and then add the stock. Bring to the boil, then reduce the heat and cover with a lid.

3 Place a frying pan over a medium heat and gently dry-roast the coconut for 2 minutes until just golden. Transfer to a blender or food processor with the sesame and poppy seeds and blend to a paste.

4 Stir the paste into the lamb shank sauce, then replace the lid and continue to cook, stirring occasionally, over a low heat for 3 hours or until the lamb is so tender that it easily falls off the bone.

5 Serve the lamb in a dish with the sauce spooned on top and finish with fine matchsticks of fresh ginger and a scattering of freshly chopped coriander.

NOTES

Deggi mirch is a full-flavoured Indian chilli powder that's relatively mild in heat. It is slightly hotter than paprika but is used more to add colour than heat to dishes. Paprika measures about 500 Scoville Heat Units (SHU) on the Scoville scale, while deggi mirch is around 1,500 to 2,000 SHU and cayenne chilli pepper can measure anything up to 50,000 SHU. When dry, deggi mirch can taste similar to paprika, but when it is fried in oil, the spice blooms to give more heat and adds a different flavour to the dish. That said, you can swap the deggi mirch for 2 tablespoons paprika and 1 tablespoon cayenne pepper.

The yellow chilli powder is difficult to substitute. Both can be found online or in specialist Indian supermarkets and stores, but if you can't find it, just add more paprika in its place.

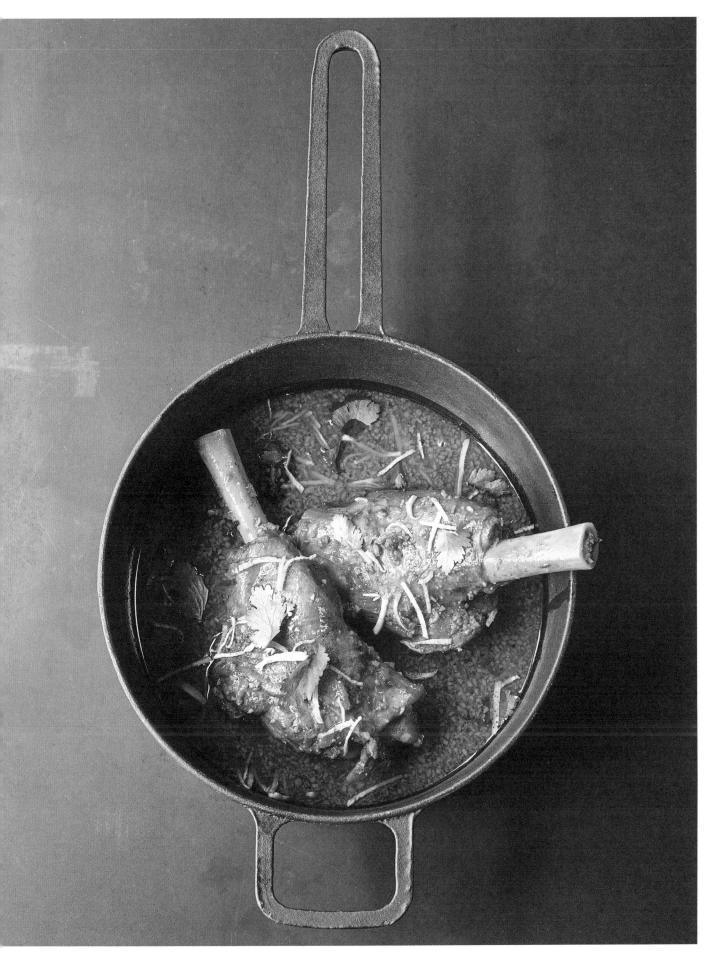

JACKFRUIT AND GUCCHI PULAO

SERVES 4–6

My grandfather used to send my mother parcels of exotic ingredients from his travels. He was a real foodie and *gucchi*, which means dried morel mushrooms, is one thing my mother loved receiving in his edible parcels. My mother is vegetarian, so ingredients like mushrooms and jackfruit – a wonderful substitute for meat – are ones she cooks with often. In India, we treat jackfruit like pulled lamb. It's beautiful in this dish.

100g ghee
2 bay leaves
1 cinnamon stick, broken in half
6 cloves
4 green cardamom pods, bruised
2 teaspoons black cumin seeds (see Tip)
2 onions, thinly sliced
300g basmati rice, rinsed and drained
50g dried morel or porcini mushrooms
150g tinned jackfruit (drained weight),
   shredded into smaller pieces
a good pinch of saffron strands (about 10),
   soaked in 1–2 tablespoons water for about
   10 minutes to release colour and aroma
100ml sunflower or rapeseed oil
sea salt

1 Heat the ghee in a flameproof casserole dish with a lid. Add the bay leaves, broken cinnamon stick, cloves, bruised cardamom pods and cumin seeds and fry for 30 seconds until fragrant.

2 Add one of the sliced onions and sauté for 5 minutes until it caramelises slightly, then add the drained rice and a good pinch of salt. Fry for a minute, then add the mushrooms, jackfruit and 400ml water.

3 When the rice mixture comes to the boil, reduce the heat, add the saffron, cover with a lid and cook for 12–15 minutes until the rice is done and the water is absorbed. Take off the heat but keep the lid on to allow the rice to steam through.

4 In a small saucepan, heat the oil over a fairly high heat until bubbling, then drop in the remaining onion slices and fry for 5 minutes until just golden and crisp. Remove with a slotted spoon, drain on kitchen paper and sprinkle with salt. Serve the rice with the crispy onions scattered over the top.

TIP
Use normal cumin seeds if you can't find black cumin.

MAA'S KASHMIRI LAMB CHOPS

SERVES 4

The 'Maa' referred to in this recipe, which has to be one of the most popular dishes on our menu, is my wife Devina's mother. She made this for me when we first met. This recipe shows you how to make the dish using a whole rack of lamb, which makes an impressive centre piece, but if you prefer you can make it with lamb cutlets on the grill instead, as we do in the restaurant.

8-bone rack of lamb,
  French-trimmed
2 tablespoons freshly squeezed
  lime juice
1 teaspoon chilli powder
1 teaspoon mango powder
  (see Note)
½ teaspoon freshly grated nutmeg
1 teaspoon freshly ground
  black pepper
½ teaspoon fenugreek seeds
sea salt

TO SERVE
lemon wedges
1 tablespoon Gunpowder
  spice blend (see page 158)
Kashmiri Radish and Beetroot Pickle
  (see page 168)

FOR THE MARINADE
2cm piece of fresh ginger, peeled
4 garlic cloves, peeled
½ green chilli
1 tablespoon mustard or
  rapeseed oil
½ teaspoon fennel seeds
¼ teaspoon ground cinnamon
100ml double cream

FOR THE CHUTNEY
2 tablespoons mint chutney
30g chopped fresh coriander
4 tablespoons Greek yogurt
2 teaspoons caster sugar
1 green chilli
2 garlic cloves, very finely chopped
2 teaspoons cumin seeds,
  toasted and ground
½ teaspoon mango powder
  (see Note)
4 tablespoons freshly squeezed
  lemon juice
sea salt, to taste

1 First make the marinade. Place the ginger, garlic, green chilli and oil in a blender or food processor and pulse until coarsely chopped. Transfer to a bowl, add the fennel seeds, cinnamon and double cream and stir to mix well.

2 Place the rack of lamb in a shallow, ovenproof dish and spoon over the creamy marinade to coat thoroughly. Marinate in the fridge for 3–4 hours before cooking.

3 To make the chutney, place all the ingredients in a blender or food processor and blend until you have a smooth, pale green mixture. Cover and chill until ready to serve. (It will keep for 3–4 days in the fridge.)

4 In a bowl, mix the lime juice, chilli powder, mango powder, nutmeg, black pepper, fenugreek and a pinch of salt. Turn the marinated lamb rack through the mix to coat.

5 Preheat your oven to 200°C/gas mark 4. Place the lamb on a baking tray, fat side up. Roast for 15–17 minutes if you like it rare, or leave for 4–5 minutes longer if you prefer if more well done. Remove from the oven, cover and leave to rest for at least 10 minutes.

6 Carve the rack between the bones into chops. Serve with a squeeze of lemon, a dusting of Gunpowder spice and a little pot of the chutney on the side, as well as some pickled radishes.

NOTE

You can buy mango powder (also called amchoor) in specialist Indian shops. It's made from tart green mangos and has a lemony flavour similar to sumac. Use sumac or lime zest if you can't find it.

ANDHRA STYLE GREY MULLET

SERVES 4

I used to work for my dad's company as a travelling salesman. Earlier in the book, I mentioned the work canteens we would stop by for food. Who knew they'd inspire so many recipes? On the whole, the canteens were quite basic. You paid just a few rupees for the basics of rice, lentils and salad, but what made the meal exciting was getting to choose a main course to go along with it. We were in Andhra when I tried a dish very similar to this one, and I never forgot it.

FOR THE MARINADE
4 grey mullet fillets
    (approx. 200g each)
1 teaspoon freshly ground
    black pepper
1 tablespoon grated fresh ginger
1 tablespoon freshly squeezed
    lemon juice
sea salt

FOR THE ANDHRA SAUCE
2 tablespoons rapeseed oil
2 teaspoons yellow mustard seeds
2 teaspoons cumin seeds
¼ teaspoon fenugreek seeds
¼ teaspoon asafoetida
12 curry leaves (fresh are best if you
    can get them, but dried are fine)
1 onion, finely chopped
1 large tomato, finely chopped
1 tablespoon ground coriander
1 tablespoon kashmiri chilli powder
    (see Note)
1½ teaspoons ground turmeric
1 teaspoon tamarind paste
150g coconut cream

FOR FRYING THE FISH
3 tablespoons rapeseed oil

1 Rinse the fish, pat dry and lay in a shallow dish. Whisk the black pepper, ginger, lemon juice and a good pinch of salt together. Pour the mix over the fish and set aside to marinate for 10 minutes.

2 In the meantime, set a saucepan with a lid over a medium heat. Add the oil for the sauce and, once hot, stir in the mustard seeds followed by cumin seeds and fenugreek seeds. When the mustard seeds start to crackle, add the asafoetida and curry leaves. Fry, stirring, for 30 seconds.

3 Fold the onion through the oil and spices and sauté for 10 minutes, or until it becomes translucent. Add the tomato, coriander, chilli powder, turmeric and 250ml water. Stir well, then cover with a lid and simmer over a medium heat for 10–15 minutes, or until the tomato has fully cooked down.

4 Remove the lid, add the tamarind pulp and mix it in well. Let it cook for a minute, then whisk in the coconut cream and cook for a further minute. Season with salt, turn off the heat and keep the sauce ready to serve.

5 Set a frying pan over a high heat to fry the fish. Add the oil and then the marinated fish, skin-side down. Fry for 3–5 minutes or until the skin is golden and crisp. Turn the fish over and cook for 2–3 minutes, or until it is just cooked through.

6 Spoon the sauce onto a large platter or serving plates and perch the fish on top, crispy skin-side up. This is delicious when garnished with crispy leeks.

NOTE

Kashmiri chillies are quite mild and have a rich, fruity taste. You can buy large bags of dried Kashmiri chillies in Indian supermarkets or online. Turn them into a chilli powder by grinding them in a coffee or spice grinder. If you can't find Kashmiri chillies or Kashmiri chilli powder, use normal chilli powder but halve the quantity.

PATURI MACCH

SERVES 4

Mustard seeds feature a lot in dishes from my home city, Kolkata. They are a really healthy spice and in this dish their heat is mellowed by the addition of fresh coconut. This nutritious dish is also perfect for the barbecue, especially if you prefer fish to meat – just skip the steaming step and place the wrapped fish on the barbecue. It might take a little longer to cook through because you're not steaming it first.

600g skinless cod fillets, cut into 4
   equal-sized pieces
4 x 23cm squares of banana leaf (see Tip)

FOR THE MARINADE
250g wholegrain mustard
2 tablespoons mustard or rapeseed oil
4 tablespoons freshly squeezed lemon juice
4 tablespoons grated fresh coconut
   (see Note on page 51) or desiccated
   coconut
2 tablespoons grated fresh ginger
4 garlic cloves, very finely chopped
1 green chilli, finely chopped
1 teaspoon Kashmiri chilli powder
   (see Note opposite)
2 tablespoons ground turmeric
1 fish or vegetable stock cube, crumbled

1 In a bowl, mix together all the marinade ingredients to a make a coarse paste.

2 Lay the fish pieces on a plate and cover with the paste until thoroughly and evenly coated. Cover and marinate in the fridge for 2–3 hours.

3 Gently warm the banana leaves over a gas flame on the hob for 10–20 seconds on each side, ensuring that they don't burn.

4 Place each marinated fish piece in the centre of a banana leaf square and fold the leaf over it like an envelope (you can tie it together with kitchen string).

5 Transfer the fish parcels to a steamer basket and steam for 25 minutes. Alternatively, gently heat 2 tablespoons water in a frying pan with a lid, then add the parcels, cover with the lid and steam them that way.

6 Place a dry griddle pan over a high heat and grill each fish parcel for 2 minutes on each side until it is charred with the griddle marks. Serve hot. This fish is lovely with rice and the Okra Raita with Pomegranate on page 180.

TIP

If you don't have any banana leaves, you can use any other edible leaf, such as a large fig leaf or wine (grape) leaves, or simply use foil or greaseproof paper.

DUM-KI-MACHLI

SERVES 4

Nirmal's face lights up when you mention this dish. He loves it so much that every time I visit him in his village he makes it for me. What makes this recipe unique is the little parcel of smouldering charcoal, which gives the dish a smoky edge as it cooks.

4 skinless sea bass fillets, cut in half
4 tablespoons ghee, plus
  ½ teaspoon for the charcoal
4 onions, thinly sliced
4 tablespoons freshly squeezed
  lemon juice
2 teaspoons finely grated ginger
1 large garlic clove,
  very finely chopped
1 teaspoon garam masala (shop-
  bought, or see page 161)
½ teaspoon carom seeds
4 green chillies (see Tip)
2 tomatoes, roughly chopped
250g Greek yogurt
coriander leaves, to garnish
sea salt

YOU'LL ALSO NEED
a piece of charcoal
2 x 12cm squares of foil

1 Place a frying pan over a medium heat, add 2 tablespoons of the ghee and cook the onions with a pinch of salt, stirring often, until golden brown – about 10 minutes.

2 Meanwhile, in a bowl, mix together the lemon juice, ginger, garlic, garam masala, carom seeds and a pinch of salt. Finely chop one of the green chillies and stir it in. Place the fish in a shallow dish and pour over the spicy lemon mixture to coat. Cover and marinate in the fridge for 30 minutes.

3 Transfer the cooked onion to a blender, add the tomatoes, yogurt and remaining green chillies (stems trimmed off first) and blend with a pinch of salt to make a fine paste.

4 Heat another 2 tablespoons ghee in a sauté pan over a medium heat. Stir in the onion paste and 200ml water and cook for 10 minutes, stirring often, then cover with a lid, reduce the heat and simmer for 5 minutes.

5 Meanwhile, heat your piece of charcoal over a gas flame on the hob. When hot, place it in a cast-iron or other heatproof dish lined with a double layer of foil. Bring the sides of the foil up to make an open parcel that you can set in the pan with the fish later.

6 Place the fish (discarding the marinade) in the sauté pan and spoon over the warm sauce.

7 Place the charcoal parcel in the centre of the pan. Pour ½ teaspoon ghee over it. Cover the pan tightly with a lid and cook the fish over a low heat for 10 minutes.

8 Serve the fish warm with the sauce, garnished with coriander leaves.

TIP

For a milder heat, discard the chilli seeds and membranes.

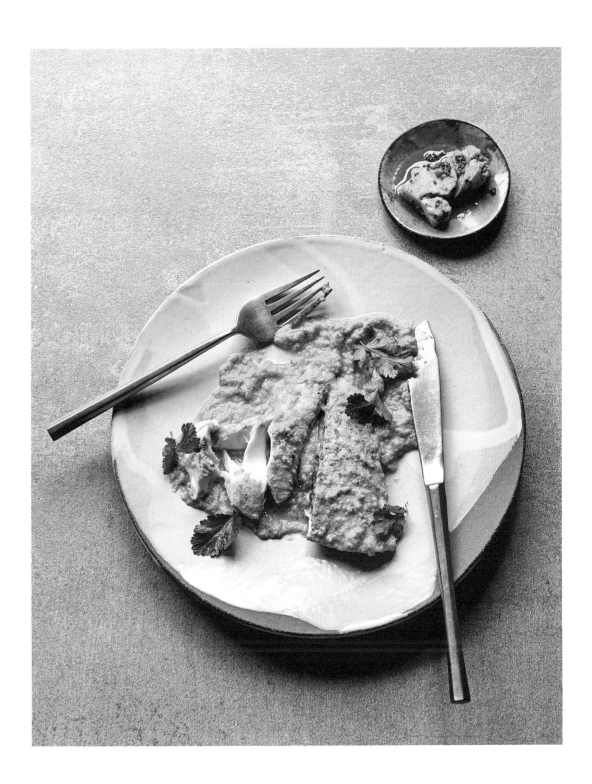

FISH POLLICHATHU

SERVES 4

I had a dish like this at one of my favourite restaurants in the south of India. The place is called Jaihind, and you could say it is the Barrafina of India. Mackerel is not a common fish in India, but you do see it on some menus. Since moving to England, both Nirmal and I rate it as one of our favourite fishes, as it takes on spices so well. Try this out – we think you'll agree.

4 whole mackerel, heads removed
1 teaspoon chilli powder
½ teaspoon ground turmeric
½ teaspoon ground coriander
½ teaspoon crushed black pepper
3 tablespoons freshly squeezed
   lemon juice
100g coconut oil or 100ml
   rapeseed oil
1 teaspoon yellow mustard seeds
1 onion, finely chopped
1 tablespoon grated fresh ginger
1 green chilli, finely chopped
4 garlic cloves, very finely chopped
1 large tomato, chopped
1 litre sunflower oil, for deep-frying
   the fish (optional)
1 tablespoon dried curry leaves
sea salt

1 Clean the mackerel and, using a sharp knife, make four diagonal, 1cm-deep slits on each side of all the fish.

2 In a shallow dish, mix together the chilli powder, turmeric, ground coriander, black pepper, lemon juice and a pinch of salt. Spoon half of this marinade into a bowl and set aside. Add the fish to the original dish and turn to coat thoroughly in the mixture. Cover and marinate in the fridge for 30 minutes.

3 Heat the coconut or rapeseed oil in a frying pan over a medium heat. Add the mustard seeds and wait for them to pop, then add the onion and cook for 5–10 minutes or until soft and a little golden. Stir in the ginger, chilli and garlic and cook for a further 2–3 minutes, then add the reserved marinade and the tomatoes and cook for 10–15 minutes or until the tomato has cooked down to a thick sauce. Add 1–2 tablespoons water if the sauce gets a little too thick. Take off the heat and cool a little, then blend in a blender or food processor to make a coarse paste.

4 Rub the paste all over the marinated fish and marinate for a further 30 minutes in the fridge.

5 Place the oil for deep-frying in a wide, deep pan and heat until bubbling. Deep-fry the fish, one at a time, for 4–5 minutes, then remove with a slotted spoon and drain on kitchen paper. Fry the curry leaves in the hot oil until crispy and drain in the same way. Alternatively, roast the fish in an oven preheated to 180°C/ gas mark 6 for 10–12 minutes, turning half way through.

6 Serve hot, scattered with the crispy curry leaves.

BLUE CRAB MALABAR CURRY

SERVES 2

The flavours of this dish are quite special, with lots of fresh coconut and a complex spice medley (but don't worry, it's easy to make). I love having this with some sort of dosa (see page 86) or appam to mop up every last drop of sauce.

300g coconut oil
2 tablespoons grated fresh ginger
5 garlic cloves, finely chopped
5 green chillies, cut in half lengthways
5 onions, thinly sliced
4 large tomatoes, finely diced
3 tablespoons ground coriander
3 tablespoons chilli powder
1 tablespoon Madras curry powder (shop-bought, or use our All-in-one Curry Powder, page 157)
1 tablespoon ground turmeric
900g raw blue or spider crab, cut into 4 pieces
150g grated fresh coconut (see Note on page 51)
1 tablespoon garam masala (shop-bought, or see page 161)
1 teaspoon freshly ground black pepper
1 teaspoon ground fennel (see Note)
3 sprigs of fresh curry leaves or 3 tablespoons dried curry leaves
5 tablespoons freshly chopped coriander
sea salt

1 Place a heavy-based sauté pan over a medium heat. Add the coconut oil, ginger, garlic and green chillies and cook, stirring, for a minute, then fold in the onions and tomatoes and sauté until both have cooked down, about 10 minutes.

2 Stir in the ground coriander, chilli powder, Madras curry powder and turmeric, then add the crab pieces and pour in enough water to just cover. Gently stir and then leave to cook for 20–25 minutes.

3 Meanwhile, in a separate, non-stick pan, dry-roast the grated coconut over a high heat until fragrant and just golden. Set aside to cool, then transfer to a blender, add 2–3 tablespoons water and blend to a smooth paste.

4 When the crab is cooked, add the roasted coconut paste, garam masala, black pepper, ground fennel, curry leaves and 3 tablespoons of the chopped coriander. Stir and simmer for 5 minutes until the sauce thickens.

5 Divide between serving plates and garnish with the remaining coriander. A few crisp fried curry leaves (see page 110) are also delicious scattered on top.

NOTE

To make 1 teaspoon ground fennel, grind 2 teaspoons fennel seeds in a spice or coffee grinder or pestle and mortar.

GRILLED SEABASS IN BANANA LEAF

This is a wonderful, light dish and great on the barbecue – especially for pescatarians. The banana leaf parcel keeps the fish wonderfully tender. Of course, you can also cook this in a frying pan, as noted below, or even roast it in the oven. No banana leaf? Just use foil or greaseproof paper, or any other edible leaf like a large fig or vine (grape) leaves. *Pictured on pages 118–119.*

2 whole sea bass, (approx. 250g each), cleaned
100g coriander, roughly chopped
10g mint leaves
4 garlic cloves, peeled
1 tablespoon grated fresh ginger
1–2 green chillies, finely chopped
½ teaspoon crushed black pepper
1 teaspoon cumin seeds
¼ teaspoon ground turmeric
2 tablespoons freshly squeezed lemon juice
20g ghee, melted
2 tablespoons Greek yogurt
2 x 30cm squares of banana leaf
your choice of raita, to serve (see pages 176–183)
sea salt

1 Take each sea bass in turn and, using a sharp knife, score the fish four times with 1cm-deep slashes across both sides.

2 Place the coriander, mint, garlic, ginger, chilli, black pepper, cumin seeds, turmeric, lemon juice and a pinch of salt in a blender or food processor and blend into a fine paste. Stir through the melted ghee and yogurt and check the seasoning.

3 Gently warm the banana leaves over a gas flame on the hob for 10–20 seconds on each side, ensuring that they don't burn.

4 Place each sea bass in the centre of a banana leaf and divide the coriander mixture between the two. Slather it all over, inside and out, then wrap the banana leaf around the fish like a parcel (you can tie it together with kitchen string). Leave to marinate for 30 minutes.

5 Preheat your oven grill to high, set a griddle pan over a high heat, or use a barbecue. When hot, grill the sea bass parcels for 7–8 minutes on both sides. Serve warm with raita on the side.

COCONUT SAMBAL-STUFFED POMFRET

SERVES 2

This recipe is from southern India, where coconut features in so many dishes. Pomfret is a celebrated fish on our shores, as it comes from the Indian Ocean. In the UK, you can use John Dory, which is found in European waters. It has a similar taste and works beautifully for this dish.

2 whole pomfret or John Dory, cleaned
rapeseed or sunflower oil, for frying
seasonal greens or salad, to serve

FOR THE MARINADE
2 tablespoons rapeseed or olive oil
1 green chilli
1 teaspoon tamarind paste
2 garlic cloves, very finely chopped
2 teaspoons grated fresh ginger
a pinch of sea salt

FOR THE COCONUT CHUTNEY
50g grated fresh coconut (see Note on
    page 51) or desiccated coconut
30g coriander leaves, freshly chopped
1 green chilli, finely chopped
1 garlic clove, very finely chopped
½ teaspoon cumin seeds
1 tablespoon diced fresh mango
½ teaspoon caster sugar
a pinch of sea salt

FOR THE COATING
50g plain flour
50g semolina
½ teaspoon ground turmeric
a pinch of chilli powder
½ teaspoon sea salt

1 Take each fish in turn and, using a sharp knife, make a deep cut to create a pocket either side of the central bone. Make four additional light cuts on both sides to help the fish cook evenly and to absorb all the flavours of the marinade.

2 Place all the marinade ingredients in a pestle and mortar and grind together to make a fine paste. Slather all over the fish until thoroughly coated. Leave to marinate for 30 minutes.

3 Wipe the pestle and mortar clean and add all the chutney ingredients, then mash with as little water as possible to make a smooth paste. Stuff the mixture into the pockets you've made in each fish.

4 Mix together all the coating ingredients on a large, flat plate, then dredge each fish in the seasoned flour and set aside.

5 Place a large frying pan over a medium heat and add enough oil to fully coat the pan. Fry one fish at a time, cooking for 4 minutes on each side or until it is cooked through – pierce the thickest piece to see if the flesh is white, a little firm and flakes from the bone. Serve straight away with a plate of seasonal greens.

MALABAR PRAWN PULAO

Nirmal and I ate this when we were travelling around the Maharashtra in Western India. Normally I prefer meat in a pulao, one that slowly cooks and renders down until it just falls apart, but this one kicks ass. The magic is in the prawn stock, which is made with the heads and shells – this is where the flavour lies.

FOR THE MARINATED PRAWNS
12 raw jumbo king prawns in their shells
5 garlic cloves, very finely chopped
1 teaspoon finely grated ginger
½ teaspoon ground turmeric
¾ teaspoon chilli powder
1 tablespoon olive or rapeseed oil
sea salt

FOR THE PRAWN STOCK
2 teaspoons ground turmeric
½ teaspoon chilli powder

FOR THE RICE
100ml olive or rapeseed oil
6 green cardamom pods
1 cinnamon stick
8 cloves
2 onions, finely chopped
2 green chillies, finely chopped
5 garlic cloves, very finely chopped
1 tablespoon grated fresh ginger
1 teaspoon ground turmeric
1 tablespoon ground coriander
4 tomatoes, finely diced
75g grated fresh coconut
   (see Note on page 51), plus extra to garnish
250g brown basmati rice, washed and soaked for 30 minutes
1 tablespoon freshly squeezed lime juice
15 mint leaves
sea salt, to taste
6 tablespoons chopped coriander, to garnish
your choice of raita, to serve
   (see pages 176–183)

1 Remove the heads and shells from the prawns and set them aside to use in the stock.

2 In a bowl, mix together the garlic, ginger, turmeric, chilli powder, oil and a pinch of salt. Fold in the shelled prawns and marinate for 30 minutes.

3 For the stock, pour 1.5 litres water into a large pan and add the prawn heads and shells along with the turmeric, chilli powder and a pinch of salt. Bring to the boil, then simmer for 15–20 minutes. Strain the stock and set aside.

4 For the rice, place a large flameproof casserole dish or pan with a lid over a high heat. Add the oil, reduce the heat and cook the cardamom, cinnamon and cloves for a minute until fragrant. Stir in the onions and gently fry for 5 minutes until lightly caramelised. Add the green chillies and cook for a minute, then add the garlic and ginger and cook, stirring, for a further minute. Fold in the turmeric and ground coriander.

5 Add the tomatoes and 1 tablespoon water to deglaze the pan. Cook for 5 minutes until the tomatoes have broken down, then stir in the grated coconut and cook for 1 minute.

6 Drain the rice and add to the pan. Turn up the heat, add the prawn stock and stir well, then cover with a lid and cook for 25 minutes until the rice is tender and the pulao looks like a loose risotto – you can add a little extra water, if necessary.

7 Stir the marinated prawns into the pulao, adding all the marinating spices, too. Fold in the lime juice and mint leaves and cook over a low heat for 5–7 minutes or until the prawns are cooked through. Season with salt and serve warm, scattered with the chopped coriander and with a bowl of raita on the side.

SWEET PLATES AND DRINKS

SWEET PLATES
AND DRINKS

In India, we love sweet things. Meals often begin with a cocktail and end with a dessert. This is certainly a tradition we like to uphold in the restaurant. The drink recipes that follow constitute a tapestry woven with ideas based on classic recipes combined with some inspired by stories of people and places, traditions and tales.

The desserts veer further away from the familiar, though all have Indian roots. You will find some of the key flavours and ingredients from the savoury chapters making a welcome return in this sweet one.

These drinks and sweet plates provide the perfect bookends for the main dishes sandwiched in this tome.

MASALA CHAAS

SERVES 2

In the north of India we have lassi, but in the south it's all about chaas, which is really refreshing. While similar to lassi, chaas is a bit lighter and can be either sweet or savoury. This one's in the latter category, and is a healthy blend of spices, herbs and yogurt. It's sure to cool you on a hot day. *Pictured on page 129 (right).*

300ml Greek or natural yogurt
¼ teaspoon black or good-quality sea salt
1 teaspoon chaat masala
1 teaspoon grated fresh ginger
1 green chilli, finely chopped
a pinch of asafoetida
1 teaspoon freshly squeezed lime juice

TO GARNISH
2 sprigs of curry leaves (fresh are best if you can get them, but dried are fine)
2 tablespoons freshly chopped coriander

1 Place all the ingredients except the curry leaves and coriander in a blender and blend until smooth. Add 100ml water to thin the mixture a little and blitz again. Chill until ready to serve.

2 To serve, divide the mixture between two glasses and garnish each with a sprig of curry leaves and some coriander leaves.

AAM PANNA
with SAFFRON AND CARDAMON

SERVES 4

Mango lassis are typically made with a sweet mango purée like this one, but the aam panna here is elevated by a beautiful blend of spices. We also serve it mixed with water instead of yogurt. If you like, it can be turned into a wonderful cocktail. I love it with vodka.

1 ripe mango, stoned and peeled
50g caster sugar
ground seeds from 6 green cardamom pods
4 saffron strands
a large pinch of freshly ground black pepper
a pinch of sea salt or black salt

1 Place the mango flesh in a blender with the sugar, cardamom, saffron, black pepper and salt and blend until smooth.

2 To serve, spoon 2–3 tablespoons of the spiced mango purée into each glass and stir in 150ml water. Adjust the concentration of the mango purée to suit your taste. Serve cold over ice.

3 You can store any remaining mango purée in an airtight container in the fridge for up to 1 week.

MINT AND APPLE LASSI

SERVES 4

We've taken a classic lassi and given it an English twist. This one is really refreshing. If you want to give it a quirky boost, swap the apple syrup for a splash of cider instead.

4 green apples, peeled, cored and chopped, plus extra to serve
650g Greek yogurt
2 teaspoons caster sugar
2 tablespoons Monin apple syrup (see Note)
15g mint leaves, plus extra sprigs to garnish
2 handfuls of ice cubes

1 Place the apple, yogurt, sugar, apple syrup, mint and ice in a high-speed blender and blitz until smooth.

2 Spoon a little chopped apple in the bottom of four glasses and pour the lassi on top. Serve straight away, garnished with a mint sprig.

NOTE

If you can't find Monin apple syrup, you can substitute it for apple juice and add a tablespoon more of caster sugar to the mixture.

COCONUT KHUS

Khus syrup is a dark green syrup with a sweet, woody flavour and scent. It is made from an extract of the roots of vetiver grass, which is closely related to sorghum but shares many characteristics with other fragrant grasses, such as lemongrass and citronella. It's really refreshing here married with coconut and vanilla ice cream. You can find khus syrup in Indian syrups or online – it's worth seeking out for its unique flavour.

500ml coconut water
150g coconut cream
1 tablespoon freshly squeezed lime juice
4 teaspoons khus syrup (see intro)
4 scoops of vanilla ice cream
4 red cherries
2 tablespoons grated fresh coconut (see Note on page 51) or desiccated coconut

1 Place the coconut water, coconut cream and lime juice in a blender and blitz together until smooth.

2 Take four tall glasses and place 1 teaspoon of khus syrup in the bottom of each. Divide the coconut mixture between the four glasses and finish with a scoop of vanilla ice cream, a red cherry and a sprinkling of grated coconut. Serve immediately.

KASHMIRI KAHWA

SERVES 2

My mum loves this drink. She lives in northern Indian, where it's much cooler, and this is what she drinks to warm her up. We call it 'cola' as it's made with brown sugar and all the spices – it's like a healthier take on the classic fizzy drink. If you prefer, you can cut the sugar in this right down or swap it out for honey.

½ cinnamon stick
2 green cardamom pods, bruised
2 cloves
2 tablespoons brown sugar
4 teaspoons green tea leaves or
    2 good-quality green tea bags
a large pinch of saffron strands, soaked
    in 1 tablespoon warm water for about
    10 minutes
2 tablespoons flaked almonds
a few mint leaves, to garnish

1 Pour 500ml water into a saucepan and place over a medium heat. Add the cinnamon, cardamom, cloves and sugar. Bring to the boil, then reduce the heat and simmer for 5 minutes.

2 Add the green tea leaves or tea bags, mix well and simmer for 4 minutes, stirring occasionally. Strain the tea, add the saffron (along with its soaking liquid) and the almond flakes and serve warm, garnished with a few mint leaves.

WATERMELON SHIKANJI

SERVES 4

This is what Indian mothers give their children instead of cola. It's a really cooling drink for when you've come home after being out in the heat.

1kg watermelon, peeled and cubed
8 teaspoons freshly squeezed lime juice
5 teaspoons honey
a pinch of black salt (optional)
1 teaspoon roasted cumin seeds, crushed
500ml sparkling or soda water
ice cubes, to serve
mint leaves, to garnish

1 Place the watermelon in a food processor or blender and blitz to a purée. Strain into a jug and then whisk in the lime juice, honey, salt and crushed cumin seeds.

2 Stir in the sparkling or soda water. Pour into four tall glasses over ice and garnish with fresh mint.

KITTY PARTY BELLINI

In India, there's a tradition between ladies who lunch. Once a month, they each take turn hosting a party at home, known as a 'Kitty' party. The 'kitty' refers to a collection of money made by the guests and paid to the host to cover the costs of holding the party. Typically, these parties start with a glass of fizz, which is the inspiration for this beautiful bellini.

150ml tablespoons mango crush (see Note)
1 tablespoon freshly chopped coriander
2 slices green chilli, plus extra to garnish
1 x 750ml bottle of Prosecco, chilled

1 Place the mango crush, coriander and chilli in a blender and blend until smooth. Divide between six champagne flutes, allowing 2 tablespoons per glass.

2 Top up with chilled prosecco. Garnish each glass with a slice of green chilli.

PANI PURI MARGARITA

Holi is a Hindu festival celebrated in the spring, also known as the 'festival of colours' or the 'festival of love'. It signifies the victory of good over evil and the arrival of spring and end of winter. For many it's a festive day to meet others, play and laugh, forget and forgive, and repair broken relationships. During the festival people throw brightly coloured paint powders at eat other, as well as water (to help the paint stick). Quite often, you'll find people lacing the water with alcohol, which has inspired this wonderful cocktail. We garnish it with crushed pani puri, a crispy Indian street food snack that is often served at Holi festivals. It makes a delicious finish.

2 tablespoons tequila
2 tablespoons Cointreau
2 tablespoons tamarind paste
1 tablespoon freshly squeezed lime juice

TO GARNISH
a pinch of Gunpowder Spice Mix (see page 158)
a thin slice of lime, twisted
a pinch of crushed puri (optional; available in Indian
    supermarkets and online)

1 Place all the ingredients except the garnishes into a cocktail shaker with some ice. Vigorously shake for 10 seconds.

2 Pour into a tumbler packed full of ice. Garnish with the Gunpowder spice, twist of lime and a dusting of crushed puri, if using.

NOTE

You can find mango crush or similar mango cocktail pre-mixed blends in most supermarkets and off-licences. Or you can make your own by puréeing the flesh from a ripe mango with 4 tablespoons water and 4 tablespoons sugar, or more or less, to taste. Store in a sealed clean bottle in the fridge for up to 3 days, or freeze until ready to use.

BOW BARRACKS GIMLET

GUNPOWDER REGIMENT

SERVES 1

SERVES 1

The Bow Barracks was a garrison's mess built for the army during World War I, located in Kolkata. If you wanted a gimlet, which is what this cocktail is based on, you'd go to the Bow Barracks.

2 tablespoons Bombay Sapphire gin
1 teaspoon freshly squeezed lime juice
2 tablespoons ginger syrup (see Note)
a thin slice of lime, twisted

1 Pour all the ingredients except the lime into a cocktail shaker with some ice. Shake for 10 seconds. Pour into cold tumblers packed with ice.

2 Garnish with the twist of lime.

Rum and coke was an army staple and the rum of choice used to be Hercules, which was distilled exclusively for the army. Old Monk was launched in the 1950s and has been an iconic drink in India ever since. It is worth seeking out a bottle if you can, but you can use another dark rum here if needed.

2 tablespoons Old Monk rum, or other dark rum
3 pinches Gunpowder Spice Mix (see page 158)
1 tablespoon freshly squeezed lime juice
200ml cola

TO GARNISH
a thin slice of lemon, twisted
a pinch of chilli powder

1 Fill a tumbler with ice. Pour in the rum, spice mix and lime. Top up with cola.

2 Garnish with the twist of lemon and a pinch of chilli powder.

NOTE

You can use the syrup from a jar of stem ginger or make up a homemade syrup by simmering 100g caster sugar with 100ml water and 4 tablespoons grated fresh ginger for 10 minutes. While still warm, strain the syrup through a sieve into a sterilised jar, filling it to the top, then seal. It will keep for 3 months in a cool place.

MASALA CHAI AND GINGER PORRIDGE

We love our tea in India, especially chai, but children aren't allowed to drink tea. This was my mother's way of letting us have a little taste of it. We serve this for breakfast, but it's so delicious that it could easily double up as a dessert.

200g bulgur wheat
1 litre almond milk
2 tablespoons ghee
2 tablespoons crystallised ginger,
  finely chopped
4 masala chai tea bags
a pinch of sea salt

TO SERVE
crushed pistachio nuts
toasted flaked almonds
fresh berries

1 Place a large saucepan with a lid over a medium heat. Add the bulgur wheat, almond milk, ghee, crystallised ginger, tea bags and a pinch of salt and bring to a gentle simmer. Reduce the heat, cover and cook for about 20 minutes, stirring occasionally, until the grains are tender and creamy. Top up with additional milk or water during cooking, if needed.

2 Lift out the tea bags and use a fork to squeeze them against the side of the pan to release all their flavour. Stir the porridge.

3 Divide the porridge between two to four bowls and serve topped with crushed pistachios, toasted flaked almonds and fresh berries.

BAKED PANEER CHEESECAKE

This is my mum's recipe. My parents travelled quite a lot and my mum would always pick up inspiration from her trips. Of course, she's given it an Indian twist by using paneer in the cheesecake and lots of cardamom. It's a stunning dessert.

300g digestive biscuits
ground seeds from 4 green
  cardamom pods
2 drops of vanilla extract
100g unsalted butter, melted

FOR THE CHEESECAKE TOPPING
400g full-fat cream cheese
175g soured cream
225g paneer, finely grated
175g caster sugar
ground seeds from 8 cardamom
  pods
1 tablespoon vanilla extract
3 medium eggs

TO SERVE
crushed pistachio nuts
mango or cherry fruit compote
  (optional)

1 Line a 23cm springform tin with greaseproof paper, allowing enough excess to overhang the edges of the tin to make it easy to remove.

2 Place the biscuits, cardamom and vanilla in a food processor and blitz until finely crushed. Add the melted butter and process until well combined and the crumbs stick together when pressed.

3 Transfer the biscuit mixture to the lined tin, using the back of a spoon to spread and press it firmly over the base and up the sides of the tin. Cover with clingfilm and place in the fridge for 30 minutes to chill.

4 Meanwhile, preheat the oven to 160°C/gas mark 3.

5 Place the cream cheese, soured cream, grated paneer, sugar, cardamom and vanilla in the cleaned bowl of the food processor and process until smooth. Whisk in the eggs, adding them one by one, until well combined.

6 Pour the cream cheese mixture into the chilled biscuit base and spread it evenly. Bake for 1 hour or until it has set completely.

7 Turn off the oven and leave the cheesecake inside until it has cooled completely before removing.

8 Chill for 4–5 hours in the fridge before removing from the tin and serving. The cheesecake is delicious topped with a scattering of crushed pistachios or with a fruit compote, like mango or cherry, served alongside.

MASALA CHAI CRÈME BRÛLÉE

MAKES 4–6

I'm a big custard fan. Anything with custard wins me over. This is just wonderful – chai goes so well in desserts. You could also add white chocolate to the mix in place of some of the sugar.

3 cloves
5 green cardamom pods
1 cinnamon stick or 1 teaspoon
   ground cinnamon
400ml double cream
100ml full-fat milk
2 Indian masala chai tea bags
½ teaspoon ground ginger
80g caster sugar, plus 4 tablespoons
   for the tops
5 large egg yolks
½ teaspoon vanilla extract
biscuits, cookies or shortbread,
   to serve (optional)

1 Preheat the oven to 160°C/gas mark 3.

2 Place the cloves, cardamom and cinnamon in a spice or coffee grinder or pestle and mortar and grind to a fine powder.

3 Pour the cream and milk into a large saucepan. Add the tea bags, ground whole spices and ginger and stir to mix well. Place the saucepan over a medium heat and bring almost to the boil, then reduce the heat and simmer for 5 minutes. Set aside to infuse further for 10 minutes, then strain the mixture through a sieve or muslin cloth.

4 In a large bowl, whisk the sugar, egg yolks and vanilla until light and creamy. Slowly pour the strained cream into the egg mixture, whisking continuously, then divide the mixture between 4–6 small ramekins.

5 Place the ramekins in a roasting tray and pour enough boiling water into the tray to reach halfway up the sides of the ramekins. Place the tray on the middle shelf of the oven and bake for 30 minutes until just set, but with a slight wobble.

6 Set aside to cool to room temperature before chilling in the fridge for a final set.

7 To finish, sprinkle enough sugar on the top of each crème brûlée to fully cover the surface of the set cream. Caramelise with either a kitchen blowtorch or under a very hot oven grill. Serve straight away or return to the refrigerator until ready to eat. Serve with your choice of biscuits, cookies or shortbread, if you like.

SPICED RHUBARB
with CREAMY SAGO CUSTARD

SERVES 4

Nirmal devised this recipe for me, as he knows how much I love custard. The rhubarb here is very much inspired by the British seasons. You get versions of rhubarb in the north of India, but it's not common.

FOR THE CUSTARD
200ml full-fat milk
200g small tapioca pearls,
    soaked overnight and drained
280ml double cream
2 medium eggs, well beaten,
    plus 1 medium egg yolk
100g white jaggery
1 vanilla pod

FOR THE SPICED RHUBARB
300ml red wine
125g soft brown sugar
grated zest of 1 orange
1 cinnamon stick
1 star anise
1 bay leaf
3 cloves
10 rhubarb stalks, trimmed and
    cut into 2.5cm pieces
a pinch of sea salt
2 tablespoons crushed
    pistachio nuts, to serve

1 First make the custard. Pour the milk into a saucepan set over a medium heat. Once it's warm but not boiling, add the tapioca pearls and simmer gently for 10 minutes or until the pearls are tender. Stir in the cream over a low heat.

2 In a bowl, whisk the whole eggs and extra egg yolk with the jaggery, then fold the mixture into the creamy tapioca. Add the vanilla pod and gently boil for 3 minutes, stirring continuously, then take off the heat. Pour into a bowl and cover the surface with clingfilm to prevent a skin forming, then leave to cool. Chill in the fridge until set.

3 For the spiced rhubarb, place the wine, brown sugar, orange zest and whole spices in a large saucepan, bring to the boil and stir until the sugar has dissolved.

4 Add the rhubarb and salt, then reduce the heat and simmer for about 9 minutes until the rhubarb is tender. With a slotted spoon, transfer the rhubarb to a shallow dish, arranging it in a single layer.

5 Boil the wine syrup in the saucepan for about 5 minutes until it reduces and thickens. Pour the syrup over the rhubarb and set aside to cool, then cover and chill in the fridge until cold.

6 Place a spoonful of compote in the bottom of four tall glasses or jars. Top with a spoonful of tapioca custard and repeat these layers until you reach the top. Finish with a scattering of crushed pistachios and serve straight away.

DARK CHOCOLATE AND CINNAMON BAR
with PASSION FRUIT SHRIKHAND SAGO

SERVES 6

Chocolate doesn't feature so much in traditional Indian desserts, but we couldn't resist orchestrating a few chocolate masterpieces for the Gunpowder menu. The chocolate bar here is like a slice of heaven – a melt-in-your mouth truffle-turned-cake that's scented with cinnamon and will make your taste buds sing. Paired with the sharp passion fruit shrikhand, which is a traditional Indian strained yogurt from Maharashtra and Gujarat, typically served at weddings, Nirmal has created a symphony of texture and flavour.

FOR THE PASSION FRUIT SHRIKHAND
500g Greek yogurt
2–3 passion fruit
50g icing sugar
¼ teaspoon ground
    cardamom seeds

FOR THE DARK CHOCOLATE
AND CINNAMON BAR
375g dark chocolate
150ml full-fat milk
475ml double cream
50g caster sugar
1 teaspoon vanilla extract
½ teaspoon ground cinnamon
2 whole medium eggs, plus 1
    medium egg yolk

TO SERVE
6 tablespoons crushed honeycomb
    (optional)

1 Pour the yogurt into a muslin cloth. Gather up the sides of the muslin and tie together with a string at the top. Hang over a bowl in the fridge for 12 hours or overnight so that all the whey drains off the yogurt, giving you a thick labneh to use as the base for the shrikhand.

2 Halve the passion fruit. Scoop out the seedy pulp from the centre and press it through a sieve to remove the seeds and give you a fresh passion fruit purée. You will need 4 tablespoons of this.

3 Once the labneh has finished straining, transfer it to a bowl (discarding the whey) and mix it with the passion fruit puree. Sift in the icing sugar and cardamom. Cover and chill until ready to serve.

4 Break the chocolate into small pieces and add to a heatproof bowl. Set the bowl over a saucepan containing a shallow pool of gently simmering water, over a low heat. Stir the chocolate often until fully melted. Set aside.

5 Pour the milk and cream into a separate saucepan with the sugar, vanilla and cinnamon. Simmer gently over a medium heat until the mixture just starts to bubble.

6 Whisk the whole eggs and egg yolk together in a large bowl. As the milk and cream mixture comes to the boil, pour it over the eggs, then whisk the mixture until smooth and thick. Fold the melted chocolate through.

7 Pour the chocolate mixture into a 23cm-square dish lined with greaseproof paper. Gently tap the dish on the work surface to release the air bubbles, then chill in the fridge for 6–12 hours or, for best results, overnight.

8 To serve, remove the chocolate bar from the fridge and cut into squares or rectangles. Serve with a heaped spoonful of the passion fruit shrikhand.

9 For an added presentational flourish, serve dusted with crushed honeycomb.

BANANA AND CURRY LEAF PARFAIT
with CHOCOLATE MOUSSE

SERVES 6

This is one of Nirmal's works of art and it's the perfect dessert to make if you're wanting to woo someone. It's a dance of three amazing flavours: bananas, chocolate and pistachio, intermingled with the fragrance of curry leaves, which work here just as a thyme or rosemary wand is waved upon a sweet pudding to cast an earthy, aromatic spell.

FOR THE BANANA AND
CURRY LEAF PARFAIT
50g peeled, ripe banana
1 tablespoon freshly squeezed
    lime juice
150g double cream
1 medium egg white
60g caster sugar
6 fried curry leaves
1 pinch curry powder (see page 157)

FOR THE DARK CHOCOLATE MOUSSE
250g dark chocolate
2 tablespoons cocoa powder
360ml thick double cream
30ml golden syrup
220g unsalted butter,
    slightly softened
¼ teaspoon ground cardamom
    seeds

FOR THE PISTACHIO CHIKKI
250g pistachios nuts
175g caster sugar
1 tablespoon ghee
a pinch of saffron strands
ground seeds of 2 green
    cardamom pods

1 In a bowl, mash or purée the banana with half the lime juice until you have a rough purée. Whip the cream until it holds its shape but is still a little soft.

2 In another, very clean bowl and using a very clean electric whisk, beat the egg white with the remaining lime juice until stiff. Slowly add the sugar until you have a stiff and shiny meringue texture.

3 Gently fold the whipped cream and egg white mixture together, then add the banana, curry leaves and curry powder and mix well.

4 Divide the mixture between six small ramekins lined with greaseproof paper. Pop into the freezer to set overnight.

5 For the mousse, finely chop the chocolate and place in a heatproof bowl with the cocoa powder. Pour the cream and syrup into a small saucepan and gently heat until it just starts to bubble. Remove from the heat and immediately pour the hot cream mixture over the chocolate. Leave to stand until the chocolate is melted, about 2–3 minutes.

6 Whisk the chocolate and cream mixture by hand until completely smooth, then set aside to cool to room temperature.

7 Once cooled, add the softened butter and ground cardamom to the chocolate mixture and beat using a handmixer, or vigorously by hand, until the mousse is completely smooth and silky.

8 Pop the mousse into the freezer for 5 minutes, then stir with a rubber spatula. Repeat three or four more times to reach the desired mousse consistency. Once nicely chilled, give the mousse a final whip until it is light and fluffy.

9 For the chikki, roughly chop the pistachios. Set a frying pan over a medium heat. Add half the ghee and, once melted, stir in the pistachios. Gently fry until lightly coloured, then spoon onto a plate to cool.

10 Return the pan to the heat and add the remaining ghee. Add the sugar and 2 teaspoons water. Stir briskly until all the sugar melts and turns a golden brown. Fold the saffron and ground cardamom into the sugar, along with the nuts.

11 Pour the mixture onto a baking tray lined with greaseproof paper. Set aside to harden. Break into pieces with a kitchen hammer.

12 To serve, remove the banana parfait from the freezer and ease from their moulds onto plates. Serve a dollop of mousse next to each parfait and decorate with a dusting of the pistachio chikki.

CHERRY AND ALMOND GHEE CAKE

SERVES 8

Ghee is a superfood. It builds the bones and can heal the gut. We've used it in this cake in place of butter, which gives the cake an extra-rich taste. We've added a little bit of plain flour to the cake to lighten it, but if you can't eat wheat or gluten, you can swap it out for more ground almonds.

2 large eggs
110g caster sugar
grated zest of 2 lemons
ground seeds from 8 green cardamom pods
110g ghee, melted
70g plain flour
150g ground almonds
35 pitted cherries, plus extra to serve
vanilla ice cream, to serve

1 Preheat the oven to 180°C/gas mark 4 and line a 25cm square tray or 15cm round cake tin with greaseproof paper.

2 In a large metal or glass bowl, whisk together the eggs, sugar, lemon zest and cardamom until light and fluffy.

3 Slowly whisk in the melted ghee and then fold in the flour and ground almonds until just combined.

4 Pour the cake mixture into the prepared tin and spread it out evenly. Dot with pitted cherries all over the surface.

5 Bake the cake in the centre of the oven for 35 minutes until golden and baked through. To test it is baked through, insert a skewer into the middle – it should come out clean.

6 Serve warm with vanilla ice cream and cherry compote or more fresh cherries.

MANGO MURABBA BAKED CHEESE CAKE

SERVES 12

Cheesecake is a family favourite – we make this all the time, and as the seasons roll by, we swap out the mango pulp and chutney for other fruity flavours like pineapple or even apples or pears. Dates also work a treat here. You can use this as a base for all sorts of incarnations.

300g digestive biscuits
2 drops of vanilla extract, or the
    seeds from 1 vanilla pod
100g unsalted butter, melted
500g full-fat soft cheese
300g soured cream
175g caster sugar
75g mango chutney
4 medium eggs
3 tablespoons mango pulp
    (see Note)

1 Line a 23cm springform tin with greaseproof paper, allowing enough excess to overhang the edges of the tin to make it easy to remove.

2 Place the biscuits and vanilla in a food processor and blitz until finely crushed. Add the melted butter and process until well combined and the crumbs stick together when pressed.

3 Transfer the biscuit mixture to the lined tin, using the back of a spoon to spread and press it firmly over the base and up the sides of the tin. Cover with clingfilm and place in the fridge for 30 minutes to chill.

4 Meanwhile, preheat the oven to 160°C/gas mark 4.

5 Place the cream cheese, soured cream, sugar and mango chutney in the cleaned bowl of the food processor and process until smooth. Whisk in the eggs, adding them one by one, until well combined.

6 Transfer 4 tablespoons of this cream cheese mixture to a separate bowl. Add the mango pulp and whisk together until well combined. Set aside. Pour into the biscuit case and spread it evenly.

7 Dollop the reserved mango and cream cheese mixture on top, using the tip of a butter knife to ripple it through and create a marble effect.

8 Bake for 1 hour or until it has set completely.

9 Turn off the oven and leave the cheesecake inside until it has cooled completely before removing. Chill for 4–5 hours in the fridge before removing from the tin and serving.

NOTE

If you can't find shop-bought mango pulp, make your own by simply pureeing the flesh of a ripe mango with a little sugar, if needed, to sweeten.

OLD MONK AND MANUKA BREAD AND BUTTER PUDDING

SERVES 6

Old Monk Rum is an iconic Indian run, launched in the 1950s. It's a full-flavoured dark rum that's aged for a minimum of seven years. It has a distinct vanilla flavour, which makes it a brilliant addition to puddings, especially this comforting bread and butter pudding, which is a marriage of two of my favourite things: custard and rum! My brother is also a sucker for this one. When he comes over from India, he'll dine in the restaurant, order this and ask for an extra portion, which he'll take back with him to devour on the flight home. The manuka here, by the way, refers to a special variety of raisin found in India. If you can't find manuka raisins, just swap for what you can source.

FOR THE BREAD PUDDING
225ml Old Monk rum,
    plus 2 tablespoons
150g raisins (use manuka raisins if
    you can find them)
1 tablespoon butter
375g double cream
450ml full-fat milk
seeds from 1 vanilla pod or
    1 teaspoon vanilla extract
3 medium eggs, plus 3 yolks
175g caster sugar
350g brioche loaf, sliced

FOR THE CINNAMON AND RUM SYRUP
200g caster sugar
1 cinnamon stick
a pinch of sea salt

1 Soak the raisins in the 225ml rum overnight. Drain and reserve both the raisins and the rum. (If you don't have time to soak them overnight, place the raisins and rum in a saucepan and simmer over a low heat for 25 minutes.)

2 Grease a 23cm square baking dish with the butter. In a deep saucepan, bring the cream, milk and vanilla to simmering point.

3 In a large bowl, whisk the whole eggs and egg yolks with the sugar and 2 tablespoons rum. Pour the simmering cream over the egg mixture and whisk until well combined to make a smooth custard.

4 Pour one third of the custard into the prepared tin. Arrange a layer of the brioche slices on top. Sprinkle half the soaked raisins over. Add another layer of custard and brioche. Pour the last third of the custard on top and sprinkle over the remaining raisins.

5 Pop the mixture in the fridge for 1 hour so that the bread can soak up all the custard.

6 Meanwhile, gently warm the reserved raisin-soaking rum in a saucepan with the sugar, cinnamon, water and a pinch of salt. Bring to the boil and boil for 2 minutes. Take off the heat.

7 Preheat the oven to 180°C/gas mark 4. Drizzle 4 tablespoons of the cinnamon and rum syrup over the top of the bread and butter pudding. Slide the pudding into the oven. Bake for 45 minutes or until the custard has set and the top is golden brown.

8 Slice and serve with vanilla ice cream, drizzled with some of the remaining cinnamon and rum syrup.

SIDES AND SPICE

SIDES
AND SPICE

There is not a single Indian dish where spices aren't the key ingredients, and while the term 'side' sounds like an afterthought, these chutneys, pickles and raitas that we've curated on the pages that follow are pretty much the pillars of our cuisine.

The recipes we've gathered together for this chapter are rich with family history, as well as flavour. Our grannies, mothers, fathers and brothers have poured their knowledge and time into perfecting the spice blends that make our food at Gunpowder so unique. Nirmal's family pickle business, and generations of home picklers in both our families, have helped mature our selection of preserves. These, and the raitas we've chosen, are ones we wouldn't dream of not having in our own home fridges.

Even if you just have one or two of these spice mixes and side dishes to hand in your kitchen, you'll be able to spin a simple dish into something sublime with a magical sprinkle, spoon, dab and dollop of these flavour-packed medleys.

ALL-IN-ONE
CURRY POWDER

MAKES ENOUGH TO FILL A 200G JAR

Some people think curry powder is a magic wand that you can add to a dish with no other spices, but really, we always use curry powder along with other layers of spices. If you cook your way through the recipes in this book, you'll get a flavour for this. We love whole spices, along with ground spice blends. This medley of spice, however, is special and makes a wonderful rub for vegetables, fish or meat.

4 tablespoons coriander seeds
3 tablespoons cumin seeds
1 tablespoon black peppercorns
seeds from 30 cardamom pods (see Tip)
5 dried bay leaves
3 cinnamon sticks
1 whole nutmeg
2 teaspoons fennel seeds
2 teaspoons cloves
2 teaspoons caraway seeds
2 teaspoons ground ginger

1 Place a frying pan over a medium heat. Add all the ingredients apart from the ground ginger and dry roast until fragrant and lightly toasted, about 2 minutes. Spread out over a plate to cool and set aside.

2 Once cool, transfer the spices to a spice or coffee grinder or pestle and mortar and grind to a fine powder. Stir the ground ginger into the spice mix, then store in an airtight container and use within 6 months.

TIP

If you don't want to deseed all those cardamom pods, simply toast and grind them whole, along with everything else, and then sieve the entire mixture to remove the husks.

GUNPOWDER SPICE MIX

South India's spice hero, this is the magic bullet for households where not everything is affordable. Sprinkle a little Gunpowder on a dish and it instantly lifts it. The spicy powder is so versatile. It can be sprinkled over dosas (see page 86) and it is awesome stirred into lentils or rice with a little oil or ghee. Try it as a dry dip for idlis and you'll be happy you did.

85g idli rice
170g urad dal
2 tablespoons chana dal
7 whole dried Kashmiri chillies
15 dried curry leaves
10g asafoetida
1 cinnamon stick
seeds from 3 green cardamom pods
2 teaspoons black peppercorns
1 teaspoon sesame seeds
a pinch of sea salt

1 Set a large frying pan over a medium heat. Add the idli rice, urad dal and chana dal and dry-roast for 2-3 minutes or until the mixture turns light brown in colour. Transfer to a plate, spread out evenly and set aside to cool.

2 Add the chillies to the same pan and dry-roast for 30 seconds.

3 Remove the chillies from the pan and add to cool with the toasted rice and dal. Mix the dried curry leaves in, spread out the mixture evenly and set aside to cool for 15 minutes.

4 Add the remaining ingredients and grind in a spice or coffee grinder or pestle and mortar to a slightly coarse powder.

5 Store in an airtight container in a cool place for up to 6 months.

NOTE

You can buy idli rice, urad dal and chana dal in specialist Indian stores, some larger supermarkets or online.

MALVANI GARAM MASALA

Garam masala hastens the metabolic system and is very much a staple of Indian cuisine, but every household will have their own recipe, and some will have various different blends of garam masala that they use for different dishes. This one has its roots in the South Konkan region of Maharashtra on the western coast of India where they eat a lot of fish. This particular blend of garam masala spices is, indeed, perfect for seafood dishes, especially mussels and crab. It's also lovely with chicken.

2 tablespoons coriander seeds
2 tablespoons black peppercorns
2 tablespoons fennel seeds
1 tablespoon cloves
1 teaspoon black cumin seeds
4 cinnamon sticks
3 blades of mace
6 bay leaves
seeds from 15 green cardamom pods
seeds from 3 black cardamom pods
2 star anise
4 dried Kashmiri red chillies

1 Place a heavy frying pan over a medium heat. When hot, add the whole spices and chillies, reduce the heat and dry-roast for 3–5 minutes or until aromatic and lightly toasted. Spread out over a plate and set aside to cool.

2 Once cool, transfer the spices and chillies to a spice or coffee grinder or pestle and mortar and grind to a fine powder. Store in an airtight container in a cool place and use within 6 months.

KOLHAPURI ROASTED MASALA

MAKES ENOUGH TO FILL A 340G JAR

This is a rich, unusual masala, as it has roasted onions in the mix. It's very much geared towards red meat and poultry. It's also lovely with game.

4 tablespoons coriander seeds
½ teaspoon cumin seeds
1 tablespoon desiccated coconut
½ teaspoon sesame seeds
½ teaspoon black peppercorns
½ cinnamon stick
2 cloves
¼ teaspoon fennel seeds
2 teaspoons rapeseed or olive oil
½ onion, thinly sliced
2 garlic cloves, thinly sliced
4 tablespoons freshly chopped
   coriander leaves
2–3 tablespoons chilli powder, to taste
sea salt

1 Place a large frying pan over a medium heat. When hot, dry-roast the coriander seeds, cumin seeds, coconut, sesame seeds, black peppercorns, cinnamon stick, cloves and fennel seeds until fragrant and lightly toasted – about 2 minutes. Spread out over a plate to cool and set aside.

2 Return the frying pan to the heat, add the oil and, when hot, fry the onion with a pinch of salt until golden and a little crisp. Add the garlic and fresh coriander and cook, stirring, for 5 minutes until everything is nicely golden and crisp. Set aside to cool completely.

3 Transfer the spices and the onion mixture to a spice or coffee grinder or pestle and mortar and grind to a fine powder. Stir the chilli powder into the spice mix, then store in an airtight container in the fridge for up to 2 weeks.

FENNEL AND CLOVE CHILLI SAUCE

MAKES 250G

This is a wonderful chilli sauce created by Nirmal. The fennel seeds and cloves give it a rounded flavour, and a hint of sweetness amongst the spice.

125g red chillies, deseeded
250g tomatoes, finely chopped
2 teaspoons chilli flakes
2 tablespoons fennel seeds
2 cloves
1 teaspoon yellow mustard seeds
75ml red wine vinegar
1 teaspoon caster sugar
2 teaspoons sea salt

1 Place the red chillies in a spice or coffee grinder or pestle and mortar and grind to a paste.

2 Place a frying pan over a medium heat, add the tomatoes and cook for about 10–15 minutes until broken down and soft. Add the chilli paste, chilli flakes, fennel seeds, cloves, mustard seeds, red wine vinegar, sugar and salt and simmer for 5 minutes. Pass through a sieve to make a smooth sauce.

3 Pour into a sterilised botted bottle and cork tightly. Store in the fridge. You can eat it straight away, but it tastes best if you wait for 1 week to let the flavours mature. Once opened, use within 2 weeks.

ANDHRA LAMB PICKLE

Every mother and grandmother in India makes pickles, as it's a way of preserving food, especially when there are no fridges. Pickles also add so much flavour to dishes – if you have a bland dish or a food you don't much like, just add pickles and it's suddenly transformed into something palatable.

1 tablespoon ground turmeric
1 tablespoon grated fresh ginger
3 garlic cloves, very finely chopped
500g boneless mutton, diced
250ml rapeseed oil
2 teaspoons chilli powder
juice of 5 lemons
sea salt

FOR THE SPICE MIX
½ teaspoon fenugreek seeds
½ teaspoon cumin seeds
½ teaspoon nigella seeds
½ teaspoon coriander seeds

1 In a bowl, mix together the turmeric, ginger and garlic with a pinch of salt. Massage the flavourings into the mutton and set aside for 30 minutes.

2 Meanwhile, place a frying pan over a medium heat. When hot, add the fenugreek, cumin, nigella and coriander seeds and dry-roast until fragrant and lightly toasted – about 2 minutes. Spread out over a plate to cool and set aside.

3 Once cool, transfer the spices to a spice or coffee grinder or pestle and mortar and grind to a fine powder. Set aside.

4 Place a saucepan over a medium heat. Add the mutton and cook in the dry pan for 10 minutes, stirring often, until nicely coloured and quite dry. Add the oil to the pan, increase the heat and fry the mutton until the meat turns golden reddish. Add the chilli powder and the spice blend you made earlier and cook, stirring, for 2 minutes.

5 Stir in the lemon juice and cook for a further 2 minutes, then take off the heat and set aside to cool. Transfer to an airtight container and store in the fridge until ready to use. It will keep for up to 2 weeks. Delicious served alongside a rice dish or with dosas, raita and chutney.

FISH PICKLE

SERVES 4–6

In India, we make this with king fish, which is very similar to mackerel. It's a sea fish found in the Indian Ocean and it's most popular in southern India, where Nirmal is from. It's an expensive fish and is often served in many fine dining restaurants in India. Here it's used in a quite a thrifty way, as a pickle, which not only preserves it so that it will for keep longer, but also helps stretch the experience of eating it as you'd only have a dollop of the pickle alongside a rice- or lentil-based meal.

1 teaspoon chilli powder
½ teaspoon ground turmeric
2 teaspoons grated fresh ginger
2 garlic cloves, very finely chopped
1 green chilli, finely chopped
2 tablespoons freshly chopped coriander
200g skinless mackerel or king fish fillet, cut into small pieces (if you prefer, you can use skin-on fish and remove the skin after cooking)
3 tablespoons rapeseed oil
1 teaspoon ground fenugreek seeds
2 tablespoons yellow mustard powder
½ teaspoon chilli powder
¼ teaspoon asafoetida
20ml bottled lemon juice or white wine vinegar
sea salt

1 In a bowl, mix together the chilli powder, turmeric, ginger, garlic, green chilli, coriander and a pinch of sea salt to make a paste. Mix the fish through the paste, ensuring that it's well coated. Marinate for 10 minutes.

2 Set a frying pan over a high heat. Add 1 tablespoon of the oil. Reduce the heat to medium and fry the marinated fish for about 5 minutes until it's cooked through. Remove from the pan and set aside until cool.

3 Place a clean frying pan over a medium heat. Add the remaining 2 tablespoons of oil. Once hot, stir in the fenugreek and mustard powder. Cook for 30 seconds, stirring continuously, then add the chilli powder and mix well.

4 Add the fried fish pieces and a pinch of salt, then mix the fish through the spices. Cook for 2 minutes, then take off the heat. Stir in the lemon juice or wine and season with salt.

5 It's ready to eat straight away, or can be packed into a sealed jar and stored in the fridge for up to a week. Eat hot or cold alongside rice, on toast, in sandwiches or with salad.

PRAWN PICKLE

SERVES 4

The tradition of making pickles is one that needs to be preserved. The art is dying out, but we're keen to keep it alive. It's the perfect way to lengthen the life of food, but pickles also add so much more texture and flavour to food.

FOR THE FRIED PRAWNS
200g raw prawns, shelled and deveined
4 tablespoons rapeseed oil
¼ teaspoon ground turmeric
sea salt

FOR THE TEMPERING SPICES
1 garlic clove, thinly sliced
6 curry leaves (fresh are best if you can get them, but dried are fine)
1 teaspoon yellow mustard seeds
¼ teaspoon cumin seeds
8 fenugreek seeds
2 dried kashmiri chillies, broken into two or three pieces

FOR THE PICKLE PASTE
1 tablespoon rapeseed oil
2 tablespoons grated fresh ginger
4 garlic cloves, very finely chopped
¼ teaspoon ground turmeric
2 teaspoons chilli powder
1 teaspoon ground coriander
½ teaspoon garam masala (shop-bought, or see page 161)
¼ teaspoon ground cumin (see Tip)
juice of 1 large lemon

1 Set a large frying pan over a medium–high heat. Add the oil, stir in the prawns and fry for 2–3 minutes until the prawns are light pink.

2 Reduce the heat to low. Fold in the ground turmeric and a pinch of salt. Fry for a minute or until the prawns are nicely coated and golden brown. Take off the heat. Remove the prawns from the oil with a slotted spoon and set aside.

3 Place the pan back on the heat, still containing the leftover oil from the prawns. Add all the tempering spices ingredients and gently fry until the garlic is light brown. Take off the heat and transfer to a plate to cool.

4 Return the pan to a medium heat. Add the oil for the pickle paste, then stir in the ginger and garlic. Fry for a minute. Add the ground turmeric and fry, stirring, for 30 seconds.

5 Take the pan off the heat and add the remaining ground spices, the tempered spice mixture and the fried prawns. Mix well to ensure that everything is well combined. Season with a pinch of sea salt, or to taste.

6 Leave to cool completely, add the lemon juice and mix well. Pack the prawn pickle into a sterilised jar and seal. Store in the fridge for up to a week.

TIP

For maximum flavour, dry-roast whole cumin seeds for 1–2 minutes, or until fragrant, and grind in a spice or coffee grinder or pestle and mortar to make your own roasted ground cumin – the difference in flavour, in comparison to shop-bought ground cumin, is remarkable.

KASHMIRI RADISH AND BEETROOT PICKLE

MAKES 2 X 340G JARS

This pickle is a brilliant staple to keep in the fridge. It's fantastic with salmon or rice, or any fish or grain-based dish. You can also make a wonderful Indian-style wrap with it together with grilled lamb and a dollop of raita wrapped in a dosa or flatbread.

350ml white wine vinegar
2 red beetroot, peeled, halved and cut into 2cm-thick wedges
2 tablespoons sea salt
2 tablespoons caster sugar
1 tablespoon fennel seeds
2 large white radishes (mooli), peeled and coarsely grated or shaved into long ribbons using a vegetable peeler

1 In a large saucepan, bring the vinegar, beetroot wedges, salt, sugar, fennel seeds, and 225ml water to a boil. Stir until the salt and sugar are fully dissolved.

2 Remove from the heat and stir in the grated radish. Pack into sterilised jars and seal.

3 Refrigerate for at least 8 hours before serving. The pickle will keep in the fridge for up to one month once opened.

RAW MANGO PICKLE

Pickles are a wonderful healing food when you're ill. Add them to plain rice or a fairly bland vegetable stew and they're fantastic – both for you and your palate. They're also great as marinades for meat, fish or paneer.

200ml rapeseed oil
4 tablespoons yellow mustard seeds, lightly crushed
1 teaspoon fenugreek seeds, crushed
2 tablespoons sea salt
2 teaspoons ground turmeric
2 tablespoons chilli powder
1 teaspoon asafoetida
250g unripe mango flesh, cut into 5cm chunks

1 Set a large saucepan over a medium heat. Add the oil, then swirl in the crushed mustard and fenugreek seeds and salt. Sauté for 2 minutes.

2 Turn off the heat and add the turmeric. Leave to cool, then add the chilli powder. Once cool, stir the diced mango through the mixture to coat in the spices.

3 Pack the pickle into a sterilised jar and store in the fridge for at least 24 hours before eating. It will keep for up to a month in the fridge.

APPLE AND DRY FRUIT MURABBA

MAKES 500G

Murabba is a sweet fruit preserve that is popular in India. This version is a recipe handed down from Nirmal's grandmother, who was a cookbook author herself. It's incredibly easy to make and a complete delight to eat at both the breakfast table or with savoury rice dishes.

4 medium-sized apples, peeled and cut into 2cm dice
60g golden sultanas
60g pitted dates, roughly chopped
60g dried apricots, halved
¼ teaspoon roasted cinnamon powder
¼ teaspoon ground mace
¼ teaspoon ground ginger
⅛ teaspoon Chinese five spice
2 tablespoon apple cider vinegar
120g brown sugar
1 tablespoon candied orange peel (or freshly grated zest of 2 oranges)
freshly grated zest of 1 lemon

1 Add the apple, dried fruits, spices and a tablespoon of the cider vinegar to a heavy-based pot or saucepan along with 4 tablespoons water. Set over a medium heat. Pop a lid on and cook for 10–15 minutes, stirring every so often, until the apples are tender. Top up with 1–2 tablespoons of water (or more or less) if the mix starts to look dry.

2 Once the apples are soft, stir in the remaining apple cider vinegar and brown sugar. Simmer over low heat, stirring constantly, until the sugar is dissolved, 2–3 minutes.

3 Fold in the candied orange peel and lemon zest and cook 1 minute longer.

4 The chutney can be eaten straight away or pack into a sterilised jar and kept for up to 2 months in the fridge. It's delicious alongside a rice pulao or you can even serve it as a compote with yogurt or porridge.

CAULIFLOWER AND MUSTARD PICKLE

Nirmal's family have a pickle business in India and this is one of his favourite pickles. I love this one, too – it's beautiful with fish.

150ml mustard or rapeseed oil
2 teaspoons fenugreek seeds
100g crushed mustard seeds
2 teaspoons ground turmeric
2 teaspoons asafoetida
250g cauliflower florets (about ½ cauliflower)
100ml freshly squeezed lemon juice
40g sea salt
1 teaspoon whole yellow mustard seeds
1 tablespoon red chilli powder

1 In a large saucepan, heat 100ml of the oil over a medium heat, then add the fenugreek seeds and crushed mustard seeds and stir well. Fold in half the turmeric and half the asafoetida. Take off the heat and immediately transfer the mixture to a food processor or blender straight away, so that you don't burn the seeds. Blend to make a paste.

2 Apply the mustard paste to the cauliflower florets. Add the lemon juice and salt.

3 Heat the remaining 50ml mustard oil in a frying pan. Add the whole mustard seeds and fry until they crackle. Fold the remaining asafoetida through. Turn off the heat and add the remaining turmeric and the chilli powder. Mix well. Add this mixture to the cauliflower and mix well.

4 Pack into a sterilised jar and seal. Store in the fridge for a week to mature before eating. Use within six weeks.

NOTE

You can buy crushed mustard seeds in Indian markets or online, but you can make your own by simply grinding whole mustard seeds (in a blender, food processor, or pestle and mortar) to a rough powder.

BHURANI RAITA

MANGO AND YOGURT DIP
(PACHADI)

SERVES 4

SERVES 4

This raita is from Hyderabadi cuisine. It combines the pungency of garlic with the aroma of coriander and the flavour of popular spices. It's super easy to make – but it tastes special and is delicious alongside biriyani and pulao.

Nirmal's mother makes this and we all go crazy for it. It's brilliant with lamb dishes or served alongside vegetarian pulao.

400g Greek yogurt
½ teaspoon black salt
¼ teaspoon chilli powder
2 tablespoons rapeseed or olive oil
5 garlic cloves, finely chopped
2 tablespoons freshly chopped coriander

1 tablespoon coconut oil
½ teaspoon yellow mustard seeds
1 teaspoon washed white urad dal
a pinch of dried chilli flakes
a pinch of asafoetida
2 sprigs of curry leaves or 14 whole curry leaves
2 shallots or 1 small onion, finely chopped
2 thumb-sized pieces of fresh turmeric,
    peeled and grated
2 green chillies, finely chopped
1 large ripe mango, stoned, peeled and diced
300g Greek yogurt
1 tablespoon freshly chopped coriander, to garnish
sea salt

1 Combine the yogurt, black salt and red chilli powder in a bowl and whisk well.

2 Set a small pan over a medium heat. Add the oil. Once the oil is hot, add the chopped garlic and fry until golden brown. Set aside to cool.

3 Once the fried garlic is cooled, set a little aside for garnish, then add the rest to the yogurt mixture, along with the oil you fried it in. Mix well and serve garnished with the reserved garlic and the coriander.

1 Place the coconut oil in a frying pan over a medium heat. When hot, add the mustard seeds and wait for them to pop, then stir in the urad dal, chilli flakes, asafoetida and curry leaves and sauté until the leaves turn crisp.

2 Add the shallots or onion, fresh turmeric and green chilli and sauté for 2–3 minutes. Stir through the mango and sauté for 3–4 minutes until it breaks down into a soft, jammy paste. Sprinkle in 1 tablespoon water, or more if necessary, and season with a pinch of salt. Take off the heat and set aside to cool.

3 In a bowl, whisk the yogurt until smooth. Fold the mango mixture through, cover and chill in the fridge until ready to use. Garnish with the freshly chopped coriander and serve with a rice or a spicy meat dish.

SPICED PINEAPPLE RAITA

SERVES 4–6

My wife Devina makes this wonderful raita. It's sweet and cooling – the perfect foil to a spicy dish like the Goan Pork (see page 93). It's also lovely with the Etti Masala (see page 76) and a dosa or rice.

500g Greek yogurt
1 teaspoon cumin seeds, toasted
4 tablespoons freshly chopped coriander
1 teaspoon chaat masala
1 green chilli, finely chopped
1 teaspoon caster sugar
200g pineapple flesh, cut into 2cm dice
a pinch of black salt or sea salt

1 In a large bowl, whisk the yogurt until smooth and then mix in half the cumin seeds, half the coriander and all the chaat masala, chilli and sugar with the salt. Hold back a few pieces of pineapple to garnish and fold the rest through the spicy yogurt.

2 Cover and chill in the fridge until ready to serve, then garnish with the remaining pineapple, cumin seeds and fresh coriander.

BOONDI AND PINK PEPPERCORN RAITA

SERVES 8

My mother makes boondi from scratch – they're little fried drops made from chickpea flour. It's a favourite snack in India, especially in my house. With the yogurt, boondi makes for a fun and delicious raita.

250g Greek yogurt
½ teaspoon cumin seeds
½ teaspoon crushed pink peppercorns
2 tablespoons coriander, finely chopped
½ teaspoon caster sugar
2 pinches of black salt or sea salt
100g boondi (see Note)

1 In a large bowl, whisk the yogurt until smooth.

2 Place a frying pan over a medium heat, add the cumin seeds and dry roast until fragrant and lightly toasted – about 1 minute.

3 Mix half the roasted cumin seeds, half the crushed pink peppercorns and half the chopped coriander into the yogurt with the sugar and salt.

4 Fold the boondi through the yogurt – it will seem like a large quantity, but it's supposed to be a thick mixture.

5 Garnish with the remaining cumin seeds, coriander and crushed pink peppercorns. Cover and chill until ready to serve.

NOTE

You can buy boondi in specialist Indian grocers or online.
If you can't find them, puffed rice will also work.

OKRA RAITA WITH POMEGRANATE

SERVES 4

This is one of Nirmal's favourite raitas – the salty cooked okra mixed with the sweet, tangy and juicy pomegranate seeds is such a great combo. This one's so nice, you could almost just eat it on its own.

18 medium-sized okra
4 tablespoons rapeseed or sunflower oil, for frying
300g Greek yogurt
½ teaspoon roasted ground cumin powder (See Tip on page 167)
¼ teaspoon chilli powder
1 teaspoon dried pomegranate seeds (optional)
½ teaspoon caster sugar
2 tablespoons fresh pomegranate seeds
sea salt

1 Wash the okra well and dry with kitchen paper, then thinly slice, discarding the woody tops.

2 Place a frying pan over a high heat. Add the oil and, when hot, shallow-fry the okra, reducing the heat a little, for about 8 minutes until golden all over. Remove with a slotted spoon and drain on kitchen paper.

3 In a bowl, whisk the yogurt until smooth. Add the roasted ground cumin powder, chilli powder and dried pomegranate seeds and mix together with the sugar and a pinch of salt. Hold back a few pieces of okra to garnish and fold the rest through the spicy yogurt.

4 Cover and chill until ready to serve, then garnish with the remaining okra and fresh pomegranate seeds.

ROASTED AUBERGINE RAITA

SERVES 4

I love this raita – it's very similar to my family's famous roasted aubergine bharta. The key is really roasting the aubergine until it's fully tender and then mashing it with a fork.

1 aubergine
300g Greek yogurt
2 tablespoons mustard or rapeseed oil
1 shallot or ¼ onion, finely diced
1 large tomato, finely diced
1 green chilli, finely chopped
6 garlic cloves, finely chopped
1 teaspoon ground cumin
4 tablespoons finely chopped coriander
juice of 1 lime
sea salt

1 Roast the aubergine over a gas flame on your hob for about 15–20 minutes, turning frequently, or in an oven preheated to 220°C/gas mark 7 for 40 minutes, until the skin is charred all over and the aubergine is tender right the way through (if you cook it in the oven, remember to prick the skin to avoid it bursting). Set aside to cool.

2 In a bowl, whisk the yogurt until smooth. Peel the burnt skin from the aubergine and remove the stem. Finely chop or mash the cooked aubergine flesh and fold into the yogurt.

3 Place a frying pan over a high heat. When hot, add the oil, turn down the heat and cook the shallot or onion, tomato, chilli and garlic with a pinch of salt until everything is nicely softened – about 10 minutes. Set aside to cool.

4 Fold the onion-tomato mixture through the yogurt with the cumin and half the coriander. Cover and chill until ready to serve and then finish with a good squeeze of lime juice, mixing it through, and garnish with the remaining coriander.

COCONUT CHUTNEY

This traditional chutney is made with fresh coconut and lentils, subtly spiced with green chillies and tempered with fresh curry leaves, giving a soothing, earthy flavour. It's the perfect accompaniment for South Indian dosas. It's also great with breakfast dishes, like the Chickpea Pancakes (see page 17), or spicier mains like the Goan Pork (see page 93). *Pictured top.*

120g grated fresh coconut (see Note on page 51)
2 tablespoons dry roasted chana dal (see Note)
½ teaspoon cumin seeds
2 green chillies, roughly chopped
1 large garlic clove, peeled
3–4 tablespoons coconut water
¾ tablespoon rapeseed or coconut oil
¼ teaspoon yellow mustard seeds
1 dried red chilli, finely sliced
¾ teaspoon washed dry urad dal (see Note)
4 curry leaves (fresh are best if you can get them, but dried are fine)
a pinch of asafoetida
sea salt

1 Place the grated coconut, roasted chana dal, cumin seeds, green chillies, garlic and coconut water in a blender and blend into a smooth paste. Spoon into a bowl and set aside.

2 Place a frying pan over a low heat, add the oil and, when hot, fry the mustard seeds, chilli and urad dal for 1–2 minutes. Add the curry leaves and asafoetida and cook for 1 minute more, stirring, until the leaves turn crisp.

3 Pour the tempering mixture over the blended chutney in the bowl. Season with salt, to taste, cover and chill in the fridge until ready to serve.

NOTE

You can buy urad dal and chana dal in specialist Indian stores, some larger supermarkets or online.

CORIANDER AND MINT CHUTNEY

SERVES 4

This is a classic for barbecued meat – or anything grilled. I also love it with grilled aubergines or tossed with roasted vegetables. You can also use a swirl to garnish soups or toss with leftover shreds of lamb and rice for an instant pulao. *Pictured on page 185.*

1 jalapeño or mild green chilli, destemmed, cut in half
    lengthways and deseeded
30g mint leaves
30g coriander
1 tablespoon freshly squeezed lemon juice
2½ teaspoons grated fresh ginger
2–3 tablespoons Greek yogurt
1 teaspoon chaat masala (see page 10)

1 Place the green chilli, mint, coriander, lemon juice and ginger in a blender and blitz to a smooth paste.

2 In a bowl, whisk 2 tablespoons of the yogurt with the chaat masala and then fold in the blended mixture. Add more yogurt if needed to make a smooth paste.

3 Cover and chill in the fridge until ready to use. It will keep for up to 3 days.

TOMATO AND CORIANDER CHUTNEY

SERVES 4

My wife loves this – it's one of her favourites. My mum makes it at home all the time. It's really delicious with the Kale and Corn Cakes (see page 18) or with simple grilled or pan-fried fish.

2 large tomatoes, roughly chopped
100g coriander, freshly chopped
2 garlic cloves, finely chopped
1 green chilli
1 teaspoon cumin seeds
1 tablespoon freshly squeezed lime juice
1 teaspoon caster sugar
sea salt

1 Place the tomatoes, coriander, garlic, green chilli and cumin seeds in a blender and blend to a fine paste – don't be tempted to add any water.

2 Transfer to a small bowl and season with the lime juice, sugar and a pinch of salt. Serve alongside any snack or starter. It will keep in the fridge for up to 3 days.

RESOURCES

We're extremely passionate about all the recipes in this book and are excited for you to experience the dishes we grew up with and love so much. The list below might help you source some of the more unusual ingredients, which may be harder to find in your local supermarket. You can order most things online, but it's also fun to visit a specialist Indian grocer or supermarket, too, if you have the time and opportunity.

TAJ STORES
Brick Lane, Shoreditch
112 Brick Lane
London E1 6RL
www.tajstores.co.uk
Tel 020 7377 0061

PLENTIFUL FOODS LTD
115–119 Drummond Street
London NW1 2HL
www.indianspiceshop.co.uk
Tel 020 7916 1831

SPICES OF INDIA
www.spicesofindia.co.uk
Tel 01202 877340

DEEPAK FOODS
2 Greaves Place
London SW17 0NE
Tel 020 8767 7819

THE SPICE SHOP
1 Blenheim Crescent
London W11 2EE
www.thespiceshop.co.uk
Tel 020 7221 4448

SPICE MOUNTAIN
Borough Market
8 Southwark Street London SE1 1TL
www.spicemountain.co.uk
Tel 020 3609 3130

INDEX

ACKNOWLEDGEMENTS

Our sincere thanks to all those who have helped to make this happen. Thank you for supporting and encouraging us in creating Gunpowder – both the book and the restaurant.

ADDITIONAL PICTURE CREDITS

Alamy Stock Photo: Julien Garcia/Hemis 174-175b. Getty Images: Jeremy Horner 63br; Richard I'Anson 62bl, 174al, 175ar; Tom Cockrem 174-175a. iStock: AAGGraphics 62al; guillermo1956 62-63a; OscarEspinosa 62-63b; RNMitra 175br.